Jezebel's Husband

&

The Sleeping Beauty

ROBERT NATHAN

Jezebel's Husband

&

The Sleeping Beauty

NEW YORK

Alfred A. Knopf

1953

L. C. catalog card number: 52–12191

THIS IS A BORZOI BOOK,
PUBLISHED BY ALFRED A. KNOPF, INC.

FIRST EDITION

Contents

Jezebel's Husband

For Sherman Marks

who got little out of all our
work together, but disappointment: to thank him for the great
and good help he gave me on
the script of *Jezebel's Husband*.

PROLOGUE

To Be Spoken By One Of The Characters

LADIES AND GENTLEMEN: you are about to witness a play on the later years of the old Biblical prophet, Jonah—on Micah, on Tiglath Pileser, and Jonah's wife Jezebel—not to be confused with the infamous queen—and his childhood love, the Lady Judith. It is also a play about God. But that doesn't mean that you have to sit there in reverent silence, with glum, closed faces, as though you were in church. Because, if God made man, He also made laughter; and if He made laughter, it was because He wanted it to be used. He teaches that way, sometimes.

I thank you.

CHARACTERS

THE PROPHET JONAH
JEZEBEL, *his wife*
   (*Not to be confused with the infamous Queen*)
JUDITH
   (*Whom he has not seen for more than twenty
   years*)
AZARIAH, *Councillor to the King*
MIRIAM, *The King's Favorite*
REBECCA
   (*her Organization sent her*)
TIGLATH PILESER
HARUBABEL, *an Assyrian Colonel*
MICAH, *a young prophet*
ASA, *a slave*
MABELE, *a slave*

ACT I

SCENE I

*Morning; the Great Hall of Jonah's palace, which is a
kind of drawing room in which most of the life of the
household takes place. It is furnished like any other Hall
or drawing room in Israel in 731 B.C.; except that there
is a chest or cabinet on one side of the room, a bench
and low table Center, and a couch of Egyptian design
at the other. Above the cabinet is a bronze plaque, com-
memorating the victory of King Jereboam over the
Aramaeans some twenty-seven years earlier. Also, in a
frame or case upon the cabinet, a large and noticeable
white feather. The palace itself is of cedar, Assyrian
motifs predominate, while through the great columns
which frame the open terrace at the rear, the distant
hills of Gad rise like a sea-blue cloud in the east.*

*There are three archways, or entrances—without doors;
to the Left, an archway opens into the dining halls and
kitchens, and to the palace entrance itself; from the
smaller archway at the Left, Rear, a short flight of steps
leads upwards to Jezebel's private balcony, with its sleep-*

5

*ing quarters and boudoir. The Right archway leads to
Jonah's quarters, and to the other rooms and offices.*

As the CURTAIN RISES, *some sight-seers are being escorted
through the palace. They come from the Right—a few
schoolboys, a handful of women with children in their
arms or at their heels, one or two elderly men—about
what you would expect to find any morning in a museum.
The group is not large, or particularly enthusiastic; one
gathers the impression that Jonah's palace does not rate
very highly as a show-place. The sight-seers are led in by
Jonah's steward and chamberlain,* ASA, *a plump Nubian
of middle age and dignified manner.*

ASA: This way . . . keep together, please. Not through
there, Miss—those are private quarters. Let's all keep
together. Now . . . you have just left the small cham-
ber to which the prophet likes to repair in the early
hours of the day. You may have noticed that it faces
east; the Lady Jezebel likes her husband to have the
morning sun. This room also faces east; but here we
enjoy the shade of the portico. The flower gardens lie
below. Note the hills of Gad in the distance; this view
is generally admired. It was chosen by the Lady
Jezebel herself; it is here the family spend their eve-
nings. The motifs on the walls commemorate Jonah's
historic visit to Nineveh, during the course of which
the good Lord entertained the prophet for seventy

two hours in the belly of a whale, down among the weeds and fishes of the sea . . .

[*A little boy whispers to his mother*]

No other prophet can make that claim. On that wall, above the cabinet, is the bronze plaque presented to Jonah by King Jereboam in honor . . .

[*The woman leans over and whispers to him. He can scarcely believe his ears*]

. . . in honor of the victory of the Aramaeans.

[*To the woman as she starts to whisper again*]

Lady! Just a moment please!

[*Continuing the discourse*]

. . . before the gates of Hamath twenty seven years ago.

[*Turning indignantly to the woman.*]

No, ma'am'. He'll just have to wait until he gets outside. This is practically holy ground!

[*Again to the group*]

And now I have here for each of you a small souvenir of your visit to the home of Jonah, the prophet. It is a scroll, with the prophet's signature . . . and a verse by the Lady Jezebel.

[*He starts to hand them out; the visitors are not at all eager for them*]

All for the sum of one obol, the proceeds of which goes to one of my lady's charities. This way out, please.

[*As he starts to shepherd the people out*]

Stay together, please. You have no obol? A shekel will do. Here you are . . . thank you, sir. Thank you . . .

thank you. *Lady!* . . . Not through there! This way
. . . this way . . . stay together please . . .

[*As* ASA *goes out,* L, *he leaves a small—a very small—*
pile of coins on top of the cabinet. A moment later,
MABELE (*pronounced Mah-belee*), *Jezebel's Nubian*
maid, comes down the steps from the balcony, Left Rear
. . . *Married to* ASA, *she is as lean as he is stout; but*
good looking and vivacious. She carries with her an ac-
count book, an ink horn, and a large quill; and after
carefully counting the coins, she proceeds to write down
the amount in her book]

This may seem a little Gothic for 731 B.C. . . . *but we*
must not be too strict; to make history appear to come
alive, we must use our own language.

[*As she is engaged in this manner, a* YOUNG MAN *enters*
quietly from the doorway, L. *One recognizes him as one*
of the sight-seers.
It is MICAH, *a young prophet from* GOLAN. *He is poor,*
and shy; but at the same time he is proud and idealistic.
He is apprehensive one moment, and impatient and cock-
sure the next; on fire with his mission, but easily doused;
awed, envious, and scornful all at once. He is what Jonah
was twenty-seven years earlier]

MICAH [*diffidently*]:   Pardon me.

MABELE [*turning in surprise*]:   What are you doing here?
Your party has left.

MICAH: I know. I . . . stayed behind.

8

MABELE [*indignantly*]:   You had no business to. Coming upon a person, besides—like that; scaring them half to death. I ought to call the guard.

MICAH: Why? I'm not doing any harm.

MABELE: What you want, anyway? Who are you?

MICAH [*with simple dignity*]:   Micah, the son of Abner, the Morasthite.

MABELE: You look like you were from the desert. You one of them minor prophets?

MICAH: I am a prophet.

MABELE [*flatly*]:   Well—the Lady Jezebel don't like to have any extra prophets hanging around here. You just better go along about your business.

MICAH: I was hoping to see Jonah.

MABELE: You might just as well go along right now, mister; he's busy. You can't see him.

MICAH: Where is he?

MABELE: He's in the garden—if you want to know; which is none of your business.

MICAH: He certainly lives in great style.

MABELE: We do all right—

MICAH: He lived in the desert too, when he was young. Do you think he'd see me if you told him I was from Golan?

MABELE: It wouldn't make any difference if you were from the Lord Almighty Himself, mister . . .

MICAH: I am.

MABELE [*dismayed*]:   Oh—oh. Don't tell *her* that.

JEZEBEL'S VOICE [*offstage*]:   Mabele! Have they gone?

MABELE [*calling*]: Yes'm—they have. [*to* MICAH] Here's the Lady Jezebel; talk to her yourself. But take my advice—figure you're going to be leaving; and when you leave—leave fast.

[JEZEBEL *enters L. rear. Jonah's wife is small and dark. She is in her late thirties, considerably younger than Jonah; she is attractive, but hard as a peach pit, and as voracious as a piranha. She enjoys her present position all the more for having been poor in her youth; and because she was overlooked as a girl, she cannot bear to be unnoticed. She is possessive, ambitious, ruthless, and efficient. She has made Jonah what he is; and means to have credit for it.*]

JEZEBEL: We simply must keep Museum hours. How was the collection?

MABELE: Small, my lady. Three obols and a shekel.

JEZEBEL [*frowning*]: Hmph! With the price of butter what it is . . . [*she sees* MICAH; *sharply*] Who is this?

MABELE: He says he's from Golan, my lady.

JEZEBEL: That's no recommendation. What does he want?

MABELE: Well . . . he want . . . What you want, Mister? Tell the lady.

MICAH: I want to see the prophet Jonah.

JEZEBEL [*coolly*]: Yes? What about?

MICAH: I'd rather—tell him—if you don't mind.

10

JEZEBEL [*carelessly*]:   Oh? Well . . . whatever you have
to say to him, you can say to me.

MICAH [*unhappily*]:   It's not—the same thing, my lady.

JEZEBEL [*sharply*]:   On the contrary, young man—it's
quite the same thing. As my husband would be the
first to tell you. What is it you want to ask him?

MICAH [*uncertainly*]:   I. . . .

MABELE: What I tell you?

MICAH [*bursting out*]:   I want an audience with the
king.

JEZEBEL: I might have known it. When he said Golan,
I should have guessed. I suppose you have a message,
or something? A prophecy? Well. . . . what?

MICAH: My message is for the king.

JEZEBEL: I suppose we're in disfavor with the Almighty
again. I must say, I find it very discouraging. Well—
what have we done *this* time? Graven images again?
You can tell me.

MICAH [*stubbornly*]:   The message is for the king.

JEZEBEL [*carelessly*]:   Then I'll see that he gets it, whatever it is.

MICAH: I must deliver it myself.

JEZEBEL: You're all the same, you young men. So important! I find it very tiresome.

MICAH: My message *is* important.

JEZEBEL: And you have to deliver it yourself—

MICAH: Yes.

JEZEBEL [*shrugging*]:   Then deliver it. Mabele—show

11

the gentleman out. The road to Bethel runs south. You
can't miss it. Good day to you.

MICAH [*miserably*]:   You know the King won't see me!

JEZEBEL: Of course he won't see you. What's more, he's
not even at court. He's hunting in the north. [*inexorably*] What was the message?

MICAH [*firmly*]:   It's for the King.

JEZEBEL: Oh . . . !

[JONAH *enters U.R., carrying a small potted geranium,
with one blossom.* JONAH *is a man now in his early fifties,
troubled, uncertain, honored,—and disappointed. He is
disappointed in life, and in himself—which is the greatest disappointment of all. He treasures his success—but
knows, in his heart, that he doesn't deserve it. For years
he has told people what they wanted to hear; he has
been a popular prophet, well paid in cash and honors.
He has done what his wife told him to—(she insisted on
it); he is rich and famous (which he certainly enjoys);
but he knows (what few suspect) that God has had
nothing whatever to say to him since the historic visit
to Nineveh. And when he remembers (as he sometimes
does) the innocence and the purity of his youth, the
taste of his success turns bitter in his mouth. Then he
would like to be like Elijah, or Elisha . . . only, not
so poor.*]

JONAH [*offstage*]:   We've got moths again, Jezebel.
[*He enters and stands a moment on the terrace.*]

There'll be worms in the apples. Hello—who's this?

JEZEBEL: A young man from the desert.

JONAH: I was afraid it was the tax collector. And the geraniums seem to have a blight . . . From the desert, did you say?

JEZEBEL: That's what I said, dear.

JONAH [*hopefully*]:   Do you know anything about moths, young man?

MICAH: We don't have moths in Golan. We have sand flies.

JONAH: Golan! You don't say! Well! Well! . . . How are you?

MICAH: Fine. How are you?

JONAH: You must stay and have a bite of lunch with us. [*aside to* JEZEBEL] Have we enough? I imagine he doesn't eat very much.

JEZEBEL [*sourly*]:   I suppose so. [*to* MABELE] Tell cook to set another place at table—below the salt. [*to* MICAH] You don't object to mutton, do you?

MICAH: Oh, no. I eat anything.

JEZEBEL [*glumly*]:   I thought so. [*to* MABELE] Come along; I want to get some artichokes out of the garden.

JONAH: Mabele—if you're going past the potting shed will you ask the gardener to start the water wheel? I'll be right there.

MABELE: I'll tell him.

[*She continues out.*]

JEZEBEL [*as she starts to follow her*]:   Jonah—how often have I asked you *not* to bring your flower pots

13

into the house? Lunch will be at one; please see that
you're ready for it. And if you see Asa anywhere, tell
him to have my market accounts ready for me . . .
And Jonah—the young man wants an introduction to
the King.

JONAH [*flatly*]:   Oh?

JEZEBEL [*with meaning*]:   He has a message.

JONAH [*unhappily*]:   Oh.

JEZEBEL [*coldly*]:   One of *those* things. Don't do anything stupid, my pet. And please get your hair cut!
[*She goes out.*]

JONAH [*unhappily*]:   No . . . no . . . I won't . . . I
mean—yes, dear . . . [*turns to* MICAH *with an as-
sumption of briskness*] A wonderful manager, my wife.
Well . . . —so you're from the Land of Tob. I know
that country very well. I used to live there— . . . Do
I know your name?

MICAH: Micah.

JONAH: Micah . . . I seem to have heard of you . . .
Well, well . . . You know I haven't been back there
in years. It was nice in the desert.

MICAH [*drily*]:   It's not too bad here.

JONAH [*a little uncomfortable*]:   I know—I know. My
wife chose it. She likes a big place. And I suppose I've
rather gotten used to it. But it was nice in the desert;
it was a good life. [*taking up* MICAH's *staff and looking at it*] I had a staff and a bowl; and in the morning
I was up before dawn. The stars were still in the sky
. . . and the air was pure and still. I didn't have a

penny—but it didn't matter. I envy you . . . What did you say your name was?

MICAH: Micah.

JONAH [*simply, with feeling*]: I envy you, Micah.

MICAH: That's hard to believe, sir.

JONAH: That's because you're young. I get homesick for the smell of the little desert flowers in the spring.

MICAH: Why not come back to us?

JONAH [*thinking he is after all making a fool of himself*]: Oh—I'm too old for that now! And besides—my wife wouldn't care for it. She doesn't like the desert. No— I'm afraid it wouldn't do. They've forgotten me back there anyway.

MICAH: They still speak of you in the schools.

JONAH [*eagerly*]: They do? What do they say?

MICAH [*hemming and hawing*]: Well . . . they—speak of you a lot!

JONAH [*dreamily*]: Really? . . . Who's there now? Amos? Obediah?

MICAH [*doubtfully*]: No—I don't think so—

JONAH: Ezekiel?

MICAH: Yes. Ezekiel's there. He's been seeing wheels in the sky. You know—disks and things. He thinks they're Seraphim.

JONAH [*happily*]: You know—they might be, at that. No reason to think the Seraphim look like us, you know. They could just as easily look like wheels . . . A strange fellow, Ezekiel. I'd love to see him again.

MICAH: I think he's preaching in Judah this season.

JONAH: Drawing good crowds?

MICAH: Oh, yes.

JONAH: You don't say! Then he might be coming up into this part of the country. [*a little enviously*] So . . . he's quite successful. [*turns to* MICAH, *then brightening up*] But that's enough about me. What about you? Tell me about yourself.

MICAH: I'm a prophet.

JONAH: I know that.

MICAH: And I have a message for the King.

JONAH: A *real* message—?

MICAH: What other kind is there?

JONAH [*embarrassed*]:   Of course . . . that's the only kind there is. I mean . . . you heard the Voice? Yourself? How do you know you did?

MICAH: How does anyone know? How did *you* know?

JONAH: Why—an angel appeared to me in a dream. And when I woke, I found beside me on the ground a white feather, which shone like the snow. [*he points to the feather in its case on the cabinet*] That's it, over there.

MICAH [*glancing at it negligently*]:   It looks like a heron feather to me.

JONAH [*with a hollow laugh*]:   That's what the High Priest said. He thought it looked a little light for an angel—a sizeable angel, that is. So he gave me an eagle's feather to carry with me—to show the King. [*with a chuckle*] They still have the wrong feather in the royal palace.

16

MICAH: Well—no bird ever dropped anything on me. I just heard the Voice, that's all.

JONAH: I know. It's a wonderful experience. But they do like proof—particularly when you're just starting out. . . . You don't want to tell me what the message was? I could . . . authenticate it, I suppose—more or less . . . professionally . . .

MICAH [*flatly*]: No.

JONAH [*regretfully*]: Well—I don't think I'd rush at it, if I were you. The King is rather upset these days, what with the trouble with Nineveh . . . I don't think this would be a good time to—to see him, at all. Jezebel doesn't think so, either—and she's usually right about those things.

MICAH [*surprised*]: You let your wife tell you what's right?

JONAH [*uncomfortably*]: My dear fellow . . . you mustn't . . . really . . . [*loyally*] My wife is a very superior woman.

MICAH: Still . . . you went to Nineveh with a message —and the whole city repented. Did your wife tell you not to go?

JONAH: No, she didn't. I didn't know her then.

MICAH [*challengingly*]: Well?

JONAH [*uncomfortably*]: It was entirely different. I went—unwillingly.

MICAH [*suddenly*]: Were you really swallowed by a whale?

JONAH: For three days and three nights. . . . I can't

17

say it was a very happy experience. As a matter of fact, I prefer not to think about it. Still, it did teach me something—something very important: that God is everywhere, even in the sea. And it taught me something else, too: that to a whale, the most divine sight in the world is another whale. You know—*that* gave me something to think about. Imagine . . . Just think of the endless creatures—God's creatures, mind you—to whom God doesn't *in the least* resemble a man. Grasshoppers, for instance. It's a strange thought, isn't it?

MICAH [*primly*]:   No Jew should have thoughts like that.

JONAH [*weakly*]:   He shouldn't?

MICAH [*severely*]:   God chose Israel—not grasshoppers.

JONAH: Yes, . . . I would have said the same thing myself, once. Do you see that plaque? [*he points to the plaque on the wall*] They gave it to me after the war with the Aramaeans. It was my first prophecy—and my most successful one. I stood up in front of Jereboam, and said: Against the insolence of Hamath, Israel shall prevail once again. And it did, too! I didn't have much style; but people seemed to like what I said . . . And then I went to Nineveh; and after that I wasn't sure about the grasshoppers. I tell you—I suffer from a plague of them. Seven-year locusts. Tax collectors, bailiffs . . . do you know what it is to be famous? It's gotten so that I'm afraid of strangers . . . afraid they hold a writ against me, afraid they want to

take my place at court . . . [*in sudden embarrassment*] . . . Forgive me—I'm being dreadfully tactless.
You wanted an audience with the King. Well—it's no
use; my wife won't let me give it to you.

MICAH: That's that, then. Well—I guess I'll be going—

JONAH [*eagerly*]: No, no—don't go; stay for lunch. It's
so nice to talk to somebody from the desert again . . .

MICAH [*getting his staff*]: I've got to get started. Bethel
is a long walk.

JONAH [*making for a little bowl of cakes, Table L.C.*]
Have something for the journey. [*proffering them*]
Some fruit cakes.

MICAH [*he's hungry*]: I don't mind . . .

[*He takes one or two.*]

JONAH [*as* MICAH *munches*]: You know, you remind
me a little of myself—long ago. Do you mind if I ask
you a personal question?

MICAH: No.

JONAH: Are you in love?

MICAH [*amazed*]: In love? With what?

JONAH: I don't know. With someone—with anyone.
When I was your age, I was in love with all the world.
I wish I could love people again—the way I did once
. . . There isn't anyone?

MICAH: No.

JONAH: I was in love with the girl next door.

MICAH: You mean the Lady Jezebel?

JONAH: No—no. Long before that. When I was young
and unknown. And poor. I wouldn't have interested

19

Jezebel then . . . No, this was something else; quite different. Her name was Judith. It didn't turn out very well; she was rich, you see . . . one of those things. Her father took her off to Tyre and married her to a Phoenician.

MICAH [*indignantly*]:   That's the wealthy class for you.

JONAH [*absently*]:   Thank you. Anyway I never saw her again . . .

[*He sighs—lost in memory and regret.*]

MICAH [*after a slight pause he brushes his hands together*]:   Thank you for the cakes. [*starting out*] I'll be on my way.

JONAH: Why don't you stay for lunch? Maybe the Lady Jezebel will change her mind . . .

MICAH [*grasping at the straw of hope*]:   Do you think so?

JONAH [*he would rather not answer that*]:   There's mutton. I fancy you don't have mutton very often in Golan. You see, I remember.

MICAH: You really want me?

JONAH: Of course.

MICAH: Well . . . all right then.

JONAH: Good . . . [*he sees the plant*] Damn. The water wheel. Look here—be a good fellow, will you, and make yourself at home for a few minutes while I run down to the potting sheds?

[MABELE *appears on the terrace, briefly.*]

MABELE: Mr. Jonah—the gardener says the budding beds are being flooded—

20

[*She disappears again.*]

JONAH [*in disgust*]:   Good Lord—wouldn't you think
  somebody could prophesy a simple thing like that?
[*He goes out after* MABELE.]

[*Left to himself,* MICAH *looks around him with discom-
fort. He is ill at ease, in the home of the most successful
of his contemporaries. He is drawn to the bowl of cakes
—he takes one or two. He peers—with obvious doubt—
at the heron's feather; he tries to read the inscription on
the plaque. He is part envious, and part contemptuous.*]

Upon this awkward reverie, enter REBECCA, MIRIAM, *and*
AZARIAH, R., *ushered in by* ASA. AZARIAH *is a Councillor
to King Pekah of Israel; he is florid, prejudiced and my-
opic—a typical demagogue and jingoist who believes
that the Jews are ever so much better than anyone else,
and who would like them to assert themselves against
Assyria—provided that God fought the War for them.*
REBECCA *is a dowdy, acidulous, middle-aged club
woman, unable to find a satisfactory cook for her household, and resentful of women's inferior place in a man-
made world.* MIRIAM *is a friend of* JEZEBEL'S, *and a favorite of the King; she is a malicious gossip, and likes
clothes. She wears a very noticeable bonnet.*]

ASA: If you will rest yourself here, Councillor, Your Excellency, I'll go in search of the master. [*to* MIRIAM]
  I know for sure the Lady Jezebel will be free presently,

Miss Miriam—just as soon as I can tell her you're here. [*with a bow to* REBECCA] And the other lady. Just make yourself comfortable. And if the Councillor will allow me . . .

[*Paying no attention to* MICAH, *he goes to the cabinet, opens it, and takes out a carafe and a silver goblet. He places them on the low table.*]

Just help yourself, Councillor, whenever you feel inclined. Now, if you'll excuse me—I'll go find the family.

[*He goes out L.R., with a disdainful look at* MICAH. AZARIAH *also glances at* MICAH, *with obvious displeasure —who glances back at him, shyly. The ladies do not appear to notice him.* AZARIAH *fills the goblet, picks it up; and walks slowly around* MICAH, *looking at him;* MICAH *follows his route with interest, and a certain self-conscious surprise. Meanwhile, the ladies are talking.*]

MIRIAM: Isn't he a lamb? That Asa? I've tried and tried to get him away from Jezebel, but he won't leave Jonah. My own steward is a horror.

REBECCA: Do you mean the steward King Pekah sent you?

MIRIAM: Yes. I think he's an Assyrian spy . . .

REBECCA: My dear—you can't be too careful—these days.

MICAH: Do you know the king, ma'am?

[MIRIAM *just gives him a puzzled look. Does she know the king? Good heavens!*]

22

AZARIAH [*to* MICAH]: Harrumph . . . Were you waiting for someone?

MICAH: Yes. Were you?

AZARIAH: Er—yes— As a matter of fact, we are.

MICAH: Then I guess we're all waiting together.

REBECCA [*to* MIRIAM]: Why don't they bring in some green girls from Ammon or Moab—the way they used to? That would solve the servant problem.

AZARIAH: My dear Rebecca, we cannot flood this country with cheap foreign labor, and still maintain our high standards of living.

REBECCA: If they don't give me a cook, I shall simply eat out.

AZARIAH: Please! Since when are our women afraid to work with their hands? Ladies, ladies— Let us rather return to the great days of Israel, to the simple virtues of our ancestors, those hewers of wood and drawers of water.

MIRIAM: What wood did you ever hew?

AZARIAH [*pompously*]: My dear Miriam . . . I was a public official at the age of twelve. At fourteen, I was an assistant tax gatherer.

MIRIAM [*dreamily*]: At fourteen, there wasn't anything I had that the tax gatherers hadn't gathered.

REBECCA: Miriam! Really!

AZARIAH [*reprovingly*]: Miriam, dear, your humor is out of place.

JEZEBEL [JEZEBEL *enters U.R.*]: Humor is never out of

23

place,—particularly in a prophet's household . . .
Miriam, darling, how nice! I thought you were in the
forest, with the king.

MIRIAM: Every time I go hunting with the king, I get
hay fever. I thought I'd spend the week-end with you,
dear.

JEZEBEL: Splendid! Azariah—you're looking very fit.
. . . And Rebecca . . . *so* nice of you to come.

REBECCA: My organization sent me—to ask your husband to address our annual meeting—

JEZEBEL: Which organization is that, my dear?

REBECCA: Our Women's National Defense League—

JEZEBEL [*slowly*]: That's one of the smaller groups, isn't
it?

REBECCA: We are prepared to offer quite a substantial
fee—

JEZEBEL [*quickly*]: We'll talk about it later. . . . You'll
all stay to lunch, of course?

REBECCA [*uncertainly*]: Oh—we didn't . . .

AZARIAH: My dear—too much trouble . . .

MIRIAM: What are you having?

JEZEBEL [*brightly*]: Mutton.

MICAH: That's right.

MIRIAM: In those little pots? With garlic and peppers
and onions and rice?

JEZEBEL [*smiling*]: Yes.

MIRIAM: We'll stay . . . How do you like my bonnet,
Jez?

JEZEBEL [*with feigned enthusiasm*]: Why, it's simply

terrific, Miriam. [*to* REBECCA] Isn't it simply terrific?
[*to* MIRIAM] I don't see how you ever think of things
like that. What . . . is it?

MIRIAM: Oh—it's just a little thing I had made up. The
main motif is the artichoke . . .

JEZEBEL: I see. What does the King think of it?

MIRIAM: He tried to eat it . . . Have you heard about
Athaliah?

JEZEBEL: No. What about her?

MIRIAM: It seems her husband—you know, Abner the
Sunamite—came home a day too soon.

JEZEBEL: No!

MIRIAM: Yes! My dear . . . *red-handed!* With an As-
syrian! Can you imagine?

AZARIAH: Jezebel . . .

REBECCA: It's bad enough with your own husband. But
with an Assyrian!

MIRIAM: They're divorcing. All she gets is ten per-
cent.

JEZEBEL [*shocked*]: Ten? The law allows her fifty!
Community property.

MIRIAM: Not when you're caught, dear.

JEZEBEL: A woman ought to look out for herself. I've
had everything in my own name, right from the beginning.

REBECCA: You deserve it, my dear. You earn every
penny of it.

AZARIAH: Jez—my dear, that reminds me—where *is*
your husband?

JEZEBEL [*vaguely*]:   Why—I don't know. [*rise*] I left
   him with this young . . . gentleman—where *is* my
   husband, young man?

MICAH [*rise*]:   He went off to do some potting.

JEZEBEL: Well, go get him for me, will you?

MICAH: Yes ma'am.

JEZEBEL: Tell him we have company.

MICAH: Yes, ma'am . . . I'll find him—

[*He gives the cakes to* AZARIAH.]

[*He goes out C.*]

AZARIAH [*with distaste*]:   Who on earth was that?

JEZEBEL: A young fellow from Golan. He has a message
   [*she takes the cakes*]—You know the sort of thing—

AZARIAH [*fretting*]:   A message . . . You discouraged
   him, of course?

JEZEBEL [*tartly*]:   What do you take me for?

AZARIAH: The King is in no mood for messages—particularly the kind these young misanthropes bring with
   them out of the desert. You—er—don't know what the
   young man's message is?

JEZEBEL: He wouldn't tell me.

AZARIAH: Mmmmmnn . . . they're all the same; each
   one has had an exclusive interview with the Most
   High. However—I must talk to you, Jezebel, before
   your husband gets back.

JEZEBEL: All three of you?

MIRIAM [*rising*]:   Come along, 'Bec—I guess we're not
   wanted—

REBECCA [*rising unwillingly*]:   Ever since I was a child,

26

I was always sent out of the room just when things began to get interesting.

JEZEBEL [*calling after them*]: If you see Jonah, tell him that lunch is almost ready.

REBECCA: I will.

MIRIAM: We will.

JEZEBEL [*turning to* AZARIAH]: Well—that's enough chit-chat. [*seriously*] What is it, Azariah?

AZARIAH: We're worried, Jezebel.

JEZEBEL: So I gathered. And you came to see—my husband?

AZARIAH: We at court have felt a certain lack of enthusiasm in your husband lately. Let's see—when was his last prophecy? Almost three years ago. On the whole, a minor effort—involving weather conditions in Gilead during a dry spell.

JEZEBEL: But it *did* rain—remember?

AZARIAH: Thirty days later. However, I didn't come here to complain of that. We have the greatest confidence in your husband, my dear; the King has often remarked that no one has given us more satisfactory prophecies, over a longer period, or more popular ones. We need one now.

JEZEBEL: In what connection—if I may ask?

AZARIAH [*uncomfortably*]: Frankly, my dear—things are not going well between ourselves and Nineveh at the moment. As a matter of fact—you may as well know it—Tiglath has mobilized half a million men at the border.

JEZEBEL [*thoughtfully*]: Then we face a war with Nineveh?

AZARIAH: Not necessarily; Tiglath will think twice about attacking us—that is, if we appear to be strong and confident. After all, we are the Chosen People; and that gives us a certain advantage. Our enemies can never be sure they won't wake up some morning on the field of battle, dead as mackerel.

JEZEBEL: Tiglath knows that, of course. As long as he thinks The Lord is on our side—whether he is or not . . .

AZARIAH: Of course it's much better if He is—but . . . things have been a little bit confused lately between us and the Almighty. Still—He *did* get us across the Red Sea—

JEZEBEL: That was long ago. Wouldn't it be simpler to raise an army and march on Nineveh?

AZARIAH: It would be unpopular. And we might never get there. And besides—we haven't any money.

JEZEBEL: Make some. You have the right of coinage and mintage.

AZARIAH: That would cause inflation. And anyway— what have we got prophets for—if they can't help us out in a fix?

JEZEBEL: I see. Of course, you could go to Amos, or Obadiah.

AZARIAH: They're not popular enough.

JEZEBEL: And of course, no one is more popular than Jonah. You should see the swarms of sight-seers every morning. And the souvenirs—we can't keep up with the demand. But it's hard to get Jonah to say anything these days . . .

AZARIAH: There's a lovely little park and a wood-lot in Sharon, with a villa, and a lake . . . three hundred acres or so . . . for someone who could persuade him . . .

JEZEBEL: I've always been fond of Sharon; it's a beautiful part of the country. I was born there . . . in rather modest circumstances. Did you say four hundred acres?—

AZARIAH: Three . . .

JEZEBEL: Jonah can be very stubborn, my friend. If he thinks he's being used.

AZARIAH [*pained*]: Please! No one intends to *use* him. All we want is someone to give the people confidence.

JEZEBEL [*thoughtfully*]: I suppose—if Jonah were to have another vision . . . here in Zebulon—

AZARIAH [*eagerly*]: Something on the constructive side—

JEZEBEL: A message of hope—

AZARIAH: Say, a word or two designed to put King Pekah in a favorable light—

JEZEBEL: Four hundred acres?

AZARIAH: Three. I might add—that little wood-lot carries with it the title of Prince—for whatever that's worth—and Princess.

JEZEBEL: It might be arranged . . . Princess of Sharon. Princess Jezebel. I wasn't always called Jezebel, you know. As a matter of fact, I was born Jehosheba. I changed my name to Jezebel when I was five— The Queen had just been killed, and eaten by the dogs, and that seemed like such a distinction somehow—you know how children are. Four hundred acres?

AZARIAH [*heavily*]:   Four hundred.

JEZEBEL: There was a nobleman in Sharon when I was a child—a petty chief, a kind of squire. I used to look at him when he came to my father's house to buy geese . . . my father was a small farmer. I'm not ashamed of it. One day he took me up with him on his horse; I sat in front of him in a cushion, and he held me. We stopped at a wooded stream, in a willow grove. I was twelve, but quite mature . . . The next day he came to buy geese as usual; but he never looked at me again. I suppose, from his point of view, there was no future in it. But it shook my confidence for a while. [*she smiles with bitter satisfaction*] The Princess Jezebel . . . of Sharon.

AZARIAH: Of and From.

JEZEBEL: I rather like that.

[JONAH, MICAH, MIRIAM, *and* REBECCA *come in from the terrace, C.*]

JONAH [*heard off as he enters*]:   I assure you ladies, nothing would give me greater pleasure. But I lead a very busy life here in Zebulon, and to appear before such a group as you describe would, I'm afraid, interfere with my work. However, I'm sure my young friend Micah, here, would be only too happy to . . .

JEZEBEL [*sharply*]:   Happy to what?

JONAH [*seeing* AZARIAH]:   Ah, your Excellency! The ladies told me you were here. Welcome to my humble palace. [*motioning to the goblet*] I see that my wife has already seen to your comfort. [*to* REBECCA] As I say —why not try Micah?

MICAH: I'd be glad to address anybody.

REBECCA [*coldly*]:   That's very kind of you, I'm sure.

JEZEBEL [*sharply to* JONAH]:   And why can't *you* address the ladies—if they want you?

JONAH: It's in Bethel, my dear.

JEZEBEL: Well? A little trip would be good for you.

JONAH: Bethel? That's not a little trip! It's a good two days.

JEZEBEL: We could break the journey at Sharon.

JONAH [*as the light dawns*]:   Oh! We.

AZARIAH: A splendid idea. And when you get to Bethel, you must stay with me.

JONAH [*feeling hemmed-in*]:   Look—you know how I feel about speeches. And besides, I can't possibly get away just now. The grapes . . .

JEZEBEL [*coldly*]:   Since when are grapes ripe at this season?

JONAH: And then—that lower field has to be manured . . . [*to* REBECCA] You've no idea the trouble it is to find good manure these days.

MIRIAM: Not at court, dear. There's any amount of it.

AZARIAH: Miriam, darling, I don't think the King would be too pleased with some of those remarks of yours—

MICAH [*impressed*]: Do you really know the King, Ma'am?

JEZEBEL [*to* JONAH, *quickly*]: You'd better think it over before you say no. A little holiday would do us both good.

REBECCA: We're not a large group, but we're quite influential—

JEZEBEL: We could stop over at my sister Naomi's—

AZARIAH: As a matter of fact, the King was saying only last week that it was a long time since he'd seen you.

JONAH [*flattered*]: Was he?

AZARIAH: I don't want to push you, old boy . . . and of course it isn't a royal command or anything like that . . . but there's an opportunity for a rather important speech just now . . .

MICAH [*no one pays any attention to him*]: I've got a message.

AZARIAH: To tell you the truth, the King has rather missed you at court lately.

JONAH [*to* MICAH, *half shamefacedly, half proud*]: You mustn't take all this too seriously. After all—I've been a prophet for a long time.

JEZEBEL [*impatiently*]: Oh, for heaven's sake—are you going to Bethel or not?

JONAH: Really, my dear—do I have to make up my mind this instant?

AZARIAH [*peaceably*]: Of course not, old boy. Of course not.

JEZEBEL [*lightly, to* REBECCA]:   You'd think I was forcing him! When it's for his own good—

AZARIAH: Oh—by the way, Jezebel . . . did I tell you that Elkiah's son, young Joshua, talked himself into a nice bit of property the other day? Stood up in the Outer Temple, and told the people in so many words to scrap their trade agreements with Tyre. Why flood the country with cheap dyes, he said: Israel has all she needs, right here at home. The Weavers and Dyers voted him a present of two hundred acres in Gilead.

JEZEBEL: Goodness! [*to* JONAH] Did you hear that, dear?

MIRIAM [*indignantly*]:   *That's* why I can't get any Tyrian purple for my hats!

REBECCA: I can tell you one thing we haven't got right here at home. We haven't got an army. Not since *some one* loaned half our chariots to Egypt. Just tell me; what happens when the Assyrians come down like a wolf on the fold?

AZARIAH [*confidently*]:   They won't.

JEZEBEL: They won't dare.

MICAH: That's not what we hear in the desert.

AZARIAH [*nettled*]:   Perhaps you haven't been listening to the right voice.

MICAH [*shocked*]:   *Please,* Mister! Whose voice do you think we hear?

AZARIAH: I know what you're going to say. But I assure you—He speaks to many different people—and often in the most contradictory terms. Would you deny that he speaks to our host, here?—to Jonah?

33

MICAH [*loyally*]:   No, of course I wouldn't deny it.

JONAH [*unhappily*]:   Really . . . Azariah—

AZARIAH: Or that his message to Jonah is any less august, or less prophetic, than to some flea-bitten hermit in a cave?

MICAH: Why flea-bitten?

JONAH: Please, Azariah—really, I . . . leave me out of this . . .

AZARIAH: Am I not right, Jezebel?

JEZEBEL: Absolutely. The whole world knows that God spoke to Jonah. [*to* MICAH] Who knows that God speaks to you?

MICAH [*simply*]:   God.

REBECCA: Hmph!

JEZEBEL [*scornfully*]:   You'll never prove anything *that* way!

AZARIAH: I have every respect for a man's opinions; what I have no use for are the soreheads and the pessimists. They make a lot of noise in the world, but they don't last. You take that fellow . . . What was his name? . . . Elijah; that was it. He won't last. I guarantee it.

MICAH: Elijah was one of the great prophets.

AZARIAH: What was so great about him? Let's take a look at the record. He opposed the King on a real estate deal. He foretold a lot of calamities. And he burned up two captains with their fifties. How did that help Israel?

MICAH: Are only the rich people Israel?

34

AZARIAH [*with deep displeasure*]: Hmmm. So you're one of those! I've seen—and heard—your kind before, young man. Loyal to anything and everything except your own country.

MICAH: That's a lie.

AZARIAH: I know you. You're one of those God-for-everybody fellows. A man who'd let his country be overrun by foreigners . . . a man who'd betray his own people for the spurious friendship of the heathen!

MICAH [*doubling up his fists*]: I ought to poke you right in the nose.

AZARIAH: I'd be delighted to have you try. I'm a little old—but I'm not afraid. I keep myself in condition.

[*He gets into the attitude of defense.*]

MICAH: But truly I am full of power by the spirit of the Lord, and of judgment, and of might!

JONAH: Gentlemen! Please!

AZARIAH: Come on, come on!

JEZEBEL: Stop it—both of you!

MICAH: Therefore I will make thee sick in smiting thee.

REBECCA [*excitedly*]: Hit him! Hit him!

MIRIAM: Which one, dear?

REBECCA [*ecstatically*]: I don't care. . . . Hit him!

AZARIAH: Come on, you hoodlum!

[*He aims a wild round-house punch at* MICAH, *who lifts his staff threateningly. He is actually nowhere near him, but the sight is too much for* AZARIAH: *He reels, clutches his heart, and gasps. At once all is confusion;* JEZEBEL *rushes to him, and holds him up anxiously;* MIRIAM *and*

35

REBECCA *cluster around him with expressions of interest;* JONAH *regards the scene somewhat dubiously, from his corner of the stage. Only* MICAH *remains aloof, lonely and impressed, gazing gratefully—but fearfully—up at heaven. They all speak at once.*]

JONAH: What is it now, Azariah?

JEZEBEL: Jonah—get him a cup of water—quickly—

MIRIAM: My goodness, he's white as a turnip.

REBECCA: Don't let him sit down—walk him around . . .

JONAH: I think some wine—

JEZEBEL [*helping* AZARIAH *to the bench*]:   Wine then—but hurry. [*to* AZARIAH] Are you all right?

REBECCA: The worst thing is to make him sit down. It's gas pressing on the diaphragm.

JONAH: Micah!

JEZEBEL [*to* JONAH]:   For heaven's sake—don't just stand there! Get him some wine!

[JONAH *goes to the cabinet, and fills a goblet with wine.*]

MIRIAM: If he has any more wine, he'll float.

AZARIAH [*gasping*]:   It's . . . nothing . . .

JEZEBEL [*easing him down onto the bench*]:   Here—lie down—stretch out.

[*She takes the goblet from* JONAH *and holds it to* AZARIAH's *lips.*]

AZARIAH [*with difficulty*]:   I'll—be—all right.

REBECCA [*to* MICAH]:   You ought to be ashamed of yourself.

MICAH: He started it.

MIRIAM: Leave the boy alone, Becky—he didn't mean anything.

JEZEBEL [*to* MICAH]:   Never mind. [to AZARIAH] A little wine . . .

[*Together they raise* AZARIAH's *head.* JONAH *stands next to the bench with the goblet.* JEZEBEL *dips her scarf in the goblet, and applies it to* AZARIAH's *forehead.*]

AZARIAH [*feeling better*]:   Help me up. Whew! That came very suddenly.

JONAH [*gently*]:   I guess we're not as young as we were, Azariah.

AZARIAH: Too close for comfort. [*to* MICAH] *You* didn't do it. [*to* JONAH] He never even hit me.

MICAH [*simply*]:   It was the Lord.

AZARIAH [*with a groan*]:   That's right . . . blame the Lord for everything—

[*He starts to rise*—JONAH *takes his arms.*]

MICAH [*declaiming*]:   Thus saith the Lord concerning the prophets that make my people err . . .

[JONAH *turns to look at* MICAH.]

AZARIAH [*disgustedly*]:   Hah!

MICAH: And the priests thereof teach for hire, and the prophets thereof divine for money—

[JONAH *looks suddenly stricken.*]

ASA [*entering L.*]:   Luncheon is served.

JEZEBEL [*with relief*]:   Thank you, Asa; we'll be with you in a moment.

REBECCA: You look awful.

AZARIAH: So do you.

[*He goes off, L., on* JONAH's *arm.*]

JEZEBEL: Well . . . shall we go in? It won't be much of a meal, I'm afraid, because we didn't really expect anyone . . . But I guess no one will starve.

[*As they go off,* MICAH *holds back, selfconsciously; he fears that he is no longer welcome as a luncheon guest.* JEZEBEL *and* REBECCA *both sweep past him;* JONAH *and* AZARIAH *have already gone in. As* MIRIAM *passes* MICAH, *she stops and smiles at him; she realizes his uncertainty and embarrassment.*]

MIRIAM: Come along . . . You're so sensitive!

[*She precedes him off, L. He follows, lonely but relieved. The stage remains empty for a moment; then* JUDITH *enters, center terrace, and stands there, looking about her. She is middle-aged, not yet grey, quite lovely; gentle, patient, and humorous. Life* (*in Tyre*) *has taught her a great deal.* JONAH *enters from R., without seeing her.*]

JEZEBEL [*voice off R.*]: I must have left it there by the bench, dear. I was using it on Azariah. Look under the table . . . we'll go ahead . . .

JONAH: All right. [*He goes to the table, and peers under it; then he looks behind the bench. As he does so, bent over with his back to the door Left, he senses someone's presence and thinks it to be* MABELE.] I'm looking for the Lady Jezebel's scarf; did you see it, Mabele? It should be here—she was using it a moment ago—

JUDITH: No, I didn't, Jonah.

[*Pause.* JONAH *is quite still.*]

JONAH [*without turning around. Softly*]:   Judith. [*He can't really believe what he thinks he hears after all these years. He turns to look at her. Now he is a little unsure.*] Judith?

JUDITH: Yes.

JONAH [*it is true*] Judith! [*then with tender affection*] Judith!

JUDITH: Jonah, after twenty-three years is that all you can say?

JONAH: Judith, how are you?

JUDITH [*a little annoyed this time by his form of greeting*]:   Fine, Jonah. How are you?

JONAH: Fine . . . [*there is a pause; then:*] Twenty-four. I didn't know you were back in Israel.

JUDITH: I have been for almost a year. I'm in Golan. I've been trying the desert and liking it—. I'm only here for a week to settle father's estate. Aren't you going to ask me to come in?

JONAH [*he motions her in*]:   Come in.

JUDITH: Yes, I thought the desert air would be good for my daughter. It's so damp in Tyre; the fogs from the sea, you know.

JONAH: So you have a daughter. You're looking wonderful, Judith. How are you?

JUDITH: Fine, thank you. You haven't changed much either, Jonah. Not half as much as I expected. You're stouter.

JONAH [*drawing himself in*]:   I lead a rather sedentary life. [*pause*] You're stouter too.

JUDITH [*draws herself in*]:   It's these clothes. Aren't you going to ask me to sit down?

JONAH: Sit down.

JUDITH [*she sits and glances around the room and then looks at* JONAH *with a frank smile*]:   It's funny, isn't it?

JONAH: What is?

JUDITH: Oh, this—seeing each other like this—my being here.

JONAH [*glancing toward the dining room*]:   It certainly is.

JUDITH: Do you have any children, Jonah?

JONAH [*pompously*]:   No, we've never been blessed that way.

JUDITH [*smiling*]:   My dear, blessed isn't just the word for it. Though I do love my girls.

JONAH: Girls? Then you have two!

JUDITH [*lightly*]:   Oh, yes.

JONAH: Well! And your husband, is he with you?

JUDITH: My husband is dead. He died over a year ago.

JONAH: Oh. I'm sorry.

[*There is a pause.*]

JUDITH: I thought of you so often, Jonah. There, in Tyre —in my big, empty palace.

JONAH: I thought about you, too. Down there at the bottom of the sea—

JUDITH [*startled*]:   Where?

JONAH: In the whale's stomach.

JUDITH [*open-mouthed*]:   Jonah were you really swallowed by a whale? [JONAH *grimaces*] I'd heard of it but I thought . . .

JONAH: Three days and three nights.

JUDITH [*amused*]:   And you thought of me. How romantic!

JONAH: You'd be surprised at the things you think about in a spot like that.

JUDITH: It took a lot of courage to stay there—

JONAH: Where else could I go?

JUDITH: How did you ever get into a thing like that? I mean—after all . . .

JONAH: It was your fault.

JUDITH: Mine?

JONAH [*sententiously*]:   When the Lord took you away from me, Judith—

JUDITH: It wasn't the Lord, dear. It was father.

JONAH: I'm afraid that God and your father were equally fateful figures to me, at the time. Anyway—I was very bitter. And the next time God gave me a message, I refused to deliver it. I ran away from Him; I took a boat to Tarshish.

JUDITH: You always were a stubborn little boy—

JONAH: I'm not stubborn.

JUDITH: Yes you are, dear. Don't you remember the time . . .

JONAH: I'm *not* stubborn. . . . Anyway—I never got there. The rest of it you know. A storm came up, they threw me into the sea . . .

JUDITH: And the whale made you famous.

JONAH: On the contrary; I assured him a place in history.

JUDITH: But it really *was* because of me, wasn't it? I don't know whether to be sorry—or proud.

JONAH: I just couldn't understand how you could—how you could *let* them . . .

JUDITH: I was only a child—I had no will of my own. You know how children are—all green dreams and hope. And father was so adamant . . . Well—in any case, I should think you'd be pleased with the way things turned out. I hear your wife is charming.

JONAH: Yes.

JUDITH: Is she pretty?

JONAH [*uncomfortably*]:   Quite.

JUDITH [*politely*]:   How nice.

[MABELE *enters from the dining room, L.*]

MABELE: Mr. Jonah, Miss Jezebel say where are you? [*looking at* JUDITH *with an air of understanding*] You want me to say you busy?

JONAH: I'll be right there. Wait a minute. [*to* JUDITH] You'll stay to lunch, won't you? [*to* MABELE]—[JUDITH *rises*] Set another place.

MABELE [*wailing*]:   Another one? My goodness—[*as she turns away*] Why don't they stay home and let the family eat?

[*She leaves.*]

JONAH [*to* JUDITH]:   It's all right, isn't it?

JUDITH [*doubtfully*]:   If you think so—Won't it seem a
bit strange—my coming in like this, out of nowhere?

JONAH [*beligerently*]:   No . . . I don't see why—

JUDITH: Well—I suppose you know best. I'd better
make myself presentable, anyway—[*She opens her
reticule, and takes out a long-handled mirror and a
rouge pot. She looks at herself in the mirror, and dabs
a little rouge on her cheeks.* JONAH *watches her in love
and wonder.*] What is she like?

JONAH: Who?

JUDITH: Your wife.

JONAH [*simply*]:   She's very capable.

JUDITH: But that's wonderful . . .

JONAH: Yes, it is . . . wonderful.

JUDITH [*smiling gently*]:   You have a great deal to be
happy for . . .

JONAH [*miserably*]:   I am happy.

JUDITH [*gently*]:   Are you? That's good. [*Returning to
her mirror again; brightly*] Do you still go back to the
desert sometimes?

JONAH: No—never. I never seem to have the time for
it anymore.

JUDITH: What a shame. The desert is so lovely in the
spring . . . you're missing all the beauty of it. I have
a little house; and a pet fox who comes every morning
for chicken wings, or a cup of milk.

JONAH: I had a fox in the desert who used to talk to me
. . . at least I thought he did. You know how you get a

43

little light-headed when you've been hungry long
enough. I remember he asked me once whether God
had a beard or a tail. I said He had a beard, of course.
I was young, you see. Now I don't know.

JUDITH: You must come some day and see my desert
house . . . you and your wife . . .

JONAH [*without much enthusiasm*]:   We'd—love to—

JUDITH: Do you remember the little secret place by the
pool where we used to meet? In father's garden?

JONAH: Yes.

JUDITH: It's all over-grown with weeds.

JONAH: No! You know—I can remember when I used
to think your father's palace was enormous.

JUDITH: Not compared to the great palaces of Sidon and
Tyre. But—you've made a great success yourself, my
dear—haven't you?

JONAH [*looks around him*]:   Yes . . . I'm a success
. . . I have a palace—as big as your father's; the King
sends his ministers to me, to ask for a happy omen, a
favorable augury. And I comply; I prophesy, I tell the
people what they like to hear, I give the King what he
wants, and I have the King's favor. But the young men,
from Tob and Golan—with their fierce, hawk-eyes and
their tattered cloaks—who haven't enough to eat, who
haven't a place to lay their heads . . . what do *they*
think of me? They come here one by one, to find a
way to get to the King—to tell him the bitter truths he
doesn't want to hear. And I put them off; it's not ex-
pedient, it's not wise, it's not smart to bother the King

just now . . . he might listen to them! And then where would Jonah be? And they go back to the desert again, with their messages unspoken—to the bare rocks and the burning skies . . . and I . . . I go back to my geraniums!

JUDITH [*faltering*]:   I don't understand—

JONAH [*inexorably*]:   When I was young, God spoke to me. He spoke to me in my dreams and in my waking hours. I had nothing—but I had that . . . even in the sorrow that sat with me like a shadow before the walls of Nineveh. What have I today? [*with a gesture toward the room*] [*heavily*] All this! . . . and God's silence.

JUDITH: But He spoke to you at Nineveh!

JONAH: Yes. And I came back to Israel a great man, because I had made Assyria repent. I've lived on that ever since.

JUDITH: He never spoke to you again?

JONAH: Never. I lost Him, Judith. Somewhere—in all this—I lost Him. He went away from me.

JUDITH: But—your prophesies? Where do they come from?

[JONAH *does not reply. In the silence,* JEZEBEL *suddenly appears in the doorway, L.*]

JONAH: Jezebel—

[JUDITH *rises; they stand and look at* JEZEBEL, *who says nothing, as the*

CURTAIN FALLS

SCENE II

The same, an hour later. Luncheon over, Asa *enters with
a tray of goblets and* Mabele *follows with a tray of fruits.*
Jezebel *and her guests are just coming out of the dining
hall L. She leads the way. They dispose themselves as
comfortably as possible in the main salon.*

JEZEBEL: It was perfectly ridiculous; the chicken ran
  right out in front of us—we couldn't possibly have
  stopped the horses. Well—what's a chicken worth?
  Even at present prices—say an obol and a half. But—
  because we looked rich . . . ten obols. I was furious—
  I wouldn't have paid it. The local magistrate wanted
  to throw us in jail!

REBECCA: The thing is—who got the chicken?

JEZEBEL: We had it for supper.

REBECCA: Fricasseed?

JEZEBEL: Stewed.

MIRIAM [Miriam *and* Micah *enter very amiable together*]: Stewed. That reminds me . . .

MICAH: Miss Miriam,—there's something I'd like to tell
  the King.

MIRIAM: You and me both, dear.

JONAH [*entering with* Azariah *and* Judith] [*to* Judith]:
  There's one thing we have better than your Phoenicians
  —our mountain wines. This little Tabor compares
  quite favorably with all but the best Syrians. [*to* Aza-

46

RIAH] It's not an *important* wine—but it has rather an
engaging little character . . . don't you think?

AZARIAH [*tasting without enthusiasm*]: Hmmmmm . . .

JONAH [*to* REBECCA]: A little wine?

REBECCA: Oh—I shouldn't! But I will—

AZARIAH [*to* JUDITH]: I think I knew your father, Mrs.
Hiram. Wasn't he Prince Ahab—of Zebulon?

JUDITH: Yes, your Excellency.

AZARIAH: Used to have a place right around here somewhere, didn't he? In Gath Hepher—? A great horse-
man, as I remember it; believed in a lot of exercise.
So do I.

JUDITH: That's right.

AZARIAH: Of course. Princess Judith . . . How *is* your
father?

JUDITH: He's dead.

AZARIAH [*startled*]: You don't say! A big, healthy fellow
like that . . . always in the saddle . . .

[*He puts his wine down hastily.*]

JEZEBEL: Jonah didn't tell me you were a princess.

JUDITH: To tell the truth, I'd almost forgotten—I've
been Mrs. Hiram for so long.

[*There is a tiny pause.*]

JONAH: Figs, any one? Figs, Rebecca? We grow them
ourselves.

REBECCA: I shouldn't.

[*But she does.*]

JONAH: Now if we could cross our own figs with the
parent fruit of Damascus—

47

AZARIAH: Make a lot of trouble, old boy, with the fig and pomegranate people.

JONAH: At least—it would be a fruitful reunion. . . . Figs, Judy . . . Judith? [JEZEBEL *looks at him sharply; he quickly offers her the bowl of fruit*] Jezebel?

JEZEBEL [*pointedly*]: Haven't we—reunions enough— without upsetting the figs?

REBECCA: I know one thing: if the Assyrians get in here, there won't be anything left to upset.

MIRIAM: You can say that again, dear.

REBECCA: The Assyrians aren't like the Egyptians—and don't you forget it. *They'd* never be satisfied with putting out a few people's eyes.

MABELE [*breaking in*]: Isn't that the truth, Miss Rebecca? That Tiglath Pileser—he's a terror. I had a cousin working for a family in Ammon, and the Assyrians came in there and put seventy thousand people to the sword.

JEZEBEL: Mabele!

MABELE: Yes ma'am! Seventy thousand. Women *and* children. Just split them right up the middle like they was lambs' kidneys.

JEZEBEL: You must excuse us, Mrs. Hiram—

JUDITH [*pallidly*]: That's quite all right—

REBECCA: We need *women* in this country. Like we had when we fought the Philistines and the Canaanites. Remember how the Lady Jael took a hammer and hit Sisera on the head with a nail? That's the kind of thing *I* mean!

JEZEBEL: Why, Becky!

REBECCA: But what can we do? We can't bear arms. We can't get in to see the king. We don't even have the right of audience any more . . .

AZARIAH [*changing the subject*]:   Hmmm . . . Let's see. You married a Phoenician, didn't you, Mrs. Hiram?

JUDITH: Yes—I did.

AZARIAH: Is he—with you?

JUDITH: I've been widowed for over a year.

JEZEBEL: Oh?

JONAH: Another fig, Rebecca?

REBECCA: I shouldn't.

AZARIAH: Wasn't there some story . . . [*he glances at* JONAH] You and our host knew each other then?

JUDITH: Yes.

AZARIAH: I see.

JONAH [*lightly*]:   Judith and I hadn't seen each other for over twenty years.

MICAH [*perks up*]:   Judith? [*to* JONAH] Oh . . . is . . . ?

JONAH: Wine, Micah?

MICAH: Well—a little—for the stomach's sake.

JUDITH: In Tyre the priests used to send up kites into the wind,—lovely big kites of different colors. They could tell things from the way they went, this way and that—in the wind. They were very clever. Once when I wanted to know when my husband was coming home from a business trip they told me . . .

JEZEBEL [*coolly*]:   Were they right?

JUDITH: Oh yes, almost.

49

MIRIAM [*drily*]:   I could use some of those kites.

ASA [*coming up quietly to* AZARIAH]:   There's a deputation of townspeople come to inquire of Your Excellency—

AZARIAH: Eh? To inquire? What the devil about?

ASA: They got this trouble on their minds—about the
war—

AZARIAH: Tell them there isn't going to be a war. Tell
them . . . Wait a minute. [*he glances thoughtfully at*
JONAH] Wait a minute. I'll talk to them. Tell them to
wait for me in the rose garden.

ASA: Yes, sir.

[*He goes out L.*]

JEZEBEL: By the way—Jonah—

JONAH: Yes, dear?

JEZEBEL: What did you do with that little pear tree you
got from Gilead?

JONAH: I'm budding it.

JEZEBEL [*pointedly*]:   He's putting a new branch on the
old roots . . . [*looking around brightly*] What do you
say we all go down to the potting sheds, and look at
the cymbidium. Mrs. Hiram . . . Your Highness?

JUDITH: Oh . . . I'm afraid I have to get home . . .

AZARIAH: Count me out, my dear. I've a little business
to do in the rose garden.

JEZEBEL [*rising*]:   Rebecca? [*to* MIRIAM, *who is trying to
sneak off*] Mamie?

REBECCA: I'd love to go with you, Lady Jezebel—

MIRIAM: Oh—all right . . . damn these country gar-

50

dens! Always, just when you want to take a nap . . .
somebody has cymbidiums. [*to* MICAH] Come along—
let's make a day of it . . . you too, little man.

MICAH: Sure. Why not?

[MICAH, MIRIAM *and* REBECCA *leave C.*]

JEZEBEL [*starting out C.*]:   You'll join us, Jonah, after
your guest has left? Don't be too long. I still have the
accounts to go over. And I'd change my gown if I were
you; the sun is quite warm. [*to* JUDITH] My husband
has rather a delicate chest, and catches cold very easily.
[*to* JONAH, *amiably*] Don't you dear? [*to* JUDITH] Goodbye, Your Highness—Come again, won't you?

[JEZEBEL *follows the others out C.* AZARIAH *rises lazily.*]

AZARIAH: Well . . . to affairs of state. I say, Jonah . . .
I'd like to see you a moment or two when I get back—

JONAH [*to* JUDITH]:   There's nothing the matter with my
chest at all.

AZARIAH: Goodbye, Lady Judith. Delighted to have seen
you again. And if ever you're in Bethel—I have a few
horses might interest you . . .

JUDITH: Goodbye, Your Excellency. It was father, with
the horses—

AZARIAH: That's right—so it was. Well . . . Good
Luck . . .

[*He goes out, C.*]

JUDITH [*smiling*]:   I'd forgotten that, about father.

JONAH: So had I.

JUDITH: Funny, isn't it . . . the things you forget.

JONAH: And remember.

JUDITH: And remember.

JONAH: I dreamed of this meeting.

JUDITH [*gently*]:   Did you?

JONAH: Often.

JUDITH [*lightly*]:   The famous prophet—and the girl who jilted him? Poor foolish me?

JONAH: Yes. A kind of glorious triumph. Only . . . it didn't turn out that way.

JUDITH: . . . It didn't turn out the way I thought it would, either.

JONAH: How did you think it would turn out?

JUDITH [*awkwardly, but with charm*]:   Oh—I don't know. There'd be the famous prophet . . . surrounded by his trophies . . . And we'd laugh about old times . . . like two old friends . . . and—well . . . I just thought it would be nice, that's all.

JONAH: When I saw you, all of a sudden it was like long ago. As though nothing had ever happened to us . . . as though all the years between had never been. The famous prophet? No. The young hermit from the desert.

JUDITH: All tattered and torn? But you were sweet.

JONAH [*behind her*]:   You know—you make a life for yourself; you close the doors on the past; and it isn't good enough. One day they swing open again anyway, and the past comes creeping out, like evening mice. The jasmine, and the twilight flute . . . the songs my mother used to sing me . . .

> *"Men—Men nobler than myself*
> *Have set me like a tree.*
> *My roots are in their dust.*
> *Let the winds blow—*
> *What is that to me?*
> *My roots are deep, I trust."*

I hadn't thought of that for a long while. Do you remember the beetle? You were sitting on the grass, talking to it—the very first time I ever saw you. I can even
tell you what you were saying: "Little beetle, tell me
what love is."

JUDITH [*smiling*]:   Imagine remembering that, all these
years!

JONAH: I remember the doves that flew around your
window . . .

JUDITH: I used to wish that you were one of them. And
that you'd light on the windowsill.

JONAH: So did I.

JUDITH: I'm rather glad you didn't!

JONAH: I'm not.

JUDITH: I had a little song, too, that I used to sing—I
don't know why.

> *"My love is a shepherd in Sharon,*
> *By rivers he waters his sheep.*
> *Blue are the waters of Sharon.*
> *Rivers of Sharon are deep."*

Oh Johnny—weren't we silly?

53

JONAH: No—we were young, and honest. Maybe the rivers in Sharon *were* blue.

JUDITH: They were, in the song.

JONAH: The song ended too soon.

JUDITH: A different kind of music . . .

JONAH: I should have stopped trying to be a prophet years ago. I should have retired. I still can.

JUDITH [*a little breathlessly*]:   They'd never let you!

JONAH: They'll let me . . .

JUDITH: What would you do?

JONAH: I could start all over again—with nothing. With a staff and a bowl. I'd come across the hills, and find you talking to a beetle. Would you feed me, Judy? If I was—thinner?

JUDITH [*troubled*]:   Jonah, dear . . . I'm an old lady—with three children—

JONAH [*baffled*]:   Three . . . Three? I thought . . .

JUDITH: Don't you see—you're only making believe that —that . . .

JONAH: Making believe what?

JUDITH: That things are like they used to be.

JONAH: They could be, Judy.

JUDITH [*alarmed*]:   Johnny!

JONAH: Yes. [*obstinately*] They could be.

JUDITH: I've got to go—

JONAH: Couldn't they be, Judy?

JUDITH [*unhappily*]:   I—I don't know what you mean, darling.

JONAH: The way they were . . . once . . .

[*He moves a little closer to her, as though to kiss her.*]

JUDITH: Johnny! Your wife!

[*He is in fact, about to kiss her,—an eventuality which she contemplates with amused dismay, and at the same time with a certain enthusiasm—when suddenly* AZARIAH *comes back from the rose garden.*]

AZARIAH [*who isn't quite sure what he has seen—or has he?*]:   Pardon me—

JONAH [*startled, he releases* JUDITH]:   Damn!

JUDITH [*she pretends not to see* AZARIAH. *With admirable aplomb, she lifts her face to* JONAH, *and points to her eye—which she blinks rapidly*]:   There—in there. I'm *sure* there's something in it. Look again.

JONAH [*it takes him a moment*]:   Where? [*he peers at the eye*] There! Oh I think I do see . . . [*he takes* JUDITH's *scarf, and twists one corner of it into a point, which he holds to her mouth*] Spit on it—

JUDITH: Ugh! [*She wets her scarf with her tongue, and* JONAH *dabs at her eye. She winces*] Mff!

JONAH: There . . . Better?

JUDITH: Ever so much better, thank you. [*to* AZARIAH, *as though she had just seen him—brightly*] Why—hello!

JONAH [*heartily*]:   Hello!

AZARIAH [*looking around behind him—are they talking to him or someone else?*]:   Hello.

JUDITH: Jonah was just taking something out of my eye.

AZARIAH: Very painful. Very painful. Did you try blowing your nose?

JUDITH: No—I didn't—

AZARIAH: Jonah—[*to* JUDITH] Forgive me, Mrs. Hiram. [*to* JONAH] But—Might I have a word with you old man?

JUDITH: I really must be going. Jonah, [*holding out her hand to him with a pretty gesture*] Thank you so much —for everything. [*to* AZARIAH] Goodbye, Your Excellency—

AZARIAH: Mrs. Hiram . . . Er—just a moment. What would you say if I asked you to help me out in a rather delicate matter?

JUDITH [*wondering*]:   Why—anything I could do, of course . . .

AZARIAH: The fact is, we've got a deputation of townspeople in the rose garden, to ask for a firm statement of intent on the part of our government in regard to the worsening relations with Nineveh.

JUDITH [*warily*]:   Oh?

JONAH [*uneasily*]:   Don't look at *me!*

AZARIAH: Don't you think it's time the country heard from its greatest prophet, Mrs. Hiram?

JUDITH [*slowly*]:   You want Jonah to prophesy something?

AZARIAH: Just a simple message of hope.

JONAH [*bitterly*]:   Hope!

JUDITH [*wonderingly*]:   You mean—as though it came from . . . ?

[*She points upward.*]

AZARIAH: Just a few words. Nothing extensive.

JONAH [*flatly*]: No.

AZARIAH [*vexed*]: What do you mean—no?

JONAH: I won't do it. I have no message of hope.

AZARIAH: Look, old man—there are people down there in that rose garden. They're worried; God knows, I don't blame them. We can't have people worried; it creates a bad situation.

JONAH [*inexorably*]: The situation is of your own making. Why come to me?

AZARIAH [*looking anxiously around*]: Where's your wife?

JONAH: What's she got to do with it?

AZARIAH: You're being very difficult, old boy. Don't you agree with me, Mrs. Hiram? He's being very difficult.

JUDITH [*slowly*]: I don't know. After all—if he doesn't *feel* anything—

[*She puts her hand up, palm up, as though feeling for rain.*]

AZARIAH: Who cares what he feels? It's what he says.

JUDITH [*shocked*]: I see.

AZARIAH: I have my job to do, and he has his. You have your job, old boy; and the country expects you to do it.

JONAH: I'm afraid the country can't ask me to do anything any more, Your Excellency. I've retired.

AZARIAH [*startled*]: What do you mean—retired?

JONAH: I'm not in prophecy any more.

AZARIAH [*aghast*]: You're not serious!

JONAH [*calmly*]: I am.

57

AZARIAH [*Sputtering*]: But my dear fellow . . . you can't!

JONAH: I'd like to know who's going to stop me!

[JEZEBEL, MIRIAM, REBECCA *enter C.*]

JEZEBEL [*to* MIRIAM]: So you see, dear, it is perfectly possible to cross the white camelia with the red . . . Hello, Your Excellency,—

AZARIAH [*pointing a trembling finger*]: He says he's retired.

JEZEBEL [*carelessly*]: Really? [*to* JUDITH] . . . Still here, Your Highness? How nice.

JUDITH: I was just going.

JEZEBEL [*to* JONAH]: You've retired? From what, dear?

JONAH [*defiantly*]: From Prophecy.

JEZEBEL [*sharply*]: Just a minute. [*to* JUDITH] Don't go, Mrs. Hiram . . . [*to* JONAH, *with sudden gentleness*] That's a little sudden, isn't it? . . . [*she glances thoughtfully at* JUDITH] Still—if that's what you want— I don't see how anyone is going to stop you.

JONAH [*to* AZARIAH]: There you are. [*to* JUDITH] You see?

JUDITH: Yes, Johnny.

JEZEBEL ["JOHNNY" *she thinks. So that's it. She flashes a veiled look at* JUDITH; *it is fairly venomous*]: It's rather too bad . . . *Johnny* . . . there was quite a little income property involved. It comes at a bad time.

JONAH [*suspiciously*]: What property?

JEZEBEL [*carelessly*]: A thousand acres or so—

JONAH: A thousand acres!

[MIRIAM *looks unbelievingly over at* AZARIAH. *He looks very unhappy; and holds up four fingers.*]

JEZEBEL: In fruit trees—and sheep—and cattle—

JONAH: Cattle!

[AZARIAH *shakes his head—but no one notices.*]

JEZEBEL: But . . . if he doesn't want it—[*looking around*] I suppose we can sell this place—though if there's a war, I don't know what we could get for it. [*to* JUDITH] You see—it costs quite a lot to keep all this up. If Jonah's going to retire, we'll have to let it go.

JUDITH [*sweetly*]:   It *is* rather large—for just the two of you . . .

JEZEBEL [*acidly*]:   Jonah always had large ideas—

AZARIAH [*aggrieved*]:   I must say, it does seem like an awful lot of fuss over very little. It isn't as though we asked for anything extensive—

MIRIAM: Just a few words! My goodness—you'd think it was a major prophecy—

JEZEBEL [*to* JONAH]:   Of course—if you don't *care* whether we're invaded or not—

JONAH: Of course I care! What do you take me for?

JEZEBEL: Did you ever stop to think what it would be like? A full scale invasion?

REBECCA: What they'd do to the women and children?

JEZEBEL: Exactly. Think what they did in Ammon.

AZARIAH: You can stop it, old boy. All we need is a word—one word . . .

MIRIAM [*brightly*]:   That we have nothing to fear!

AZARIAH: That the Holy One of Israel is with us—

REBECCA: He'd better be! We have no chariots!

[MICAH *comes on C.; and stands listening.*]

AZARIAH: They want a sign, Jonah. Down there in the rose garden . . . They're asking for it.

[MICAH *looks off in wonder toward the garden. He sees a dawn of hope for him.*]

JONAH [*crying out*]:   But I have no sign!

MIRIAM: Nonsense! Anybody can have a sign.

JUDITH [*unhappily*]:   Oh Johnny!

JONAH: Please! Please! What makes you think the Lord is on our side? He hasn't spoken to me for years! He may have gone to Timbuctoo, for all I know!

JEZEBEL [*exasperated*]:   Oh, for heaven's sake—

AZARIAH: But Jonah—my dear fellow . . . it doesn't matter *where* He is—as long as they think He's *here!* That's the whole point!

JONAH: But don't you see? It isn't *true!*

MIRIAM [*disgusted*]:   Who cares?

AZARIAH: As a matter of fact, old man . . . It's time you made a little comeback here . . . You don't want to retire on a downbeat! You want a real success—like the Aramaean campaign—and then you can retire in a blaze of glory. Well—here's your chance; one word from you—the right word, mind you—and we're out of the woods. Tiglath will never cross the frontier—if the Lord is with Israel!

JONAH [*slowly*]:   I had a dream last night. I dreamt I died; and the great wind of space came over me. And I rode the wind. By myself. All alone. All by myself.

60

AZARIAH: Splendid. And are you *sure* the King wasn't with you?

JONAH: I was alone.

AZARIAH: Still—you have to admit—it wouldn't change it very much to have King Pekah there too. You see the point, don't you? The King rides the whirlwind—that's good. That's perfect.

JEZEBEL: You see? It's all there.

MIRIAM: It's a natural—that's what it is.

[JONAH *looks helplessly at* JUDITH.]

JUDITH [*softly*]: Do what you *want* to do, Jonah!

JONAH [*glumly*]: The King wasn't there. I was all alone.

JEZEBEL [*furiously*]: Look. For twenty years I've kept you the number one prophet in this Kingdom—in the world, practically. When time after time you'd have given it away to the first tramp from the desert who had a message for the King. Do you think it was easy . . . covering up for you when you made a fool of yourself? Like that time with the rains? Do you think I haven't worried? Do you think I haven't lain awake nights, adding up bills, figuring up accounts? So that you could play the great man? And now—when everything is in your hands—a thousand acres in Sharon, a title, everything—you want to give it up and retire! Well—retire then—and to hell with you. But do it afterwards.

[A *murmur is heard from the crowd outside.*]

JEZEBEL: Do you hear? They want a sign.

JONAH: A sign? Where from? My heart? Or must I put

it together in my brain like pieces of a puzzle? What has a prophet to do with signs—with omens and auguries—Leave that to the Priests and the sooth-sayers. No! I won't.

[*He sits, and puts his head down in his hands.*]

[*The murmur is repeated. On the terrace,* MICAH *makes up his mind; he moves so as to face the rose garden, and holds up his hand.*]

MICAH: My people! [*There is a surprised sound from the unseen deputation. On the stage,* JEZEBEL, MIRIAM, REBECCA *and* AZARIAH *turn toward* MICAH. *They can scarcely believe their eyes.* JUDITH *watches* JONAH, *anxiously; he doesn't lift his head.*] I will give you a sign. I have heard a Voice—the Voice of the Lord!

JEZEBEL: Good God!

MICAH: And the Voice said to me: the good man is perished out of the earth, and there is none upright among men. They all lie in wait for blood; they hunt every man his brother with a net.

[*There is a murmur of dismay from the crowd.*]

MIRIAM [*in consternation*]:   What's he saying?

MICAH: For the rich men thereof are full of violence and the inhabitants thereof have spoken lies, and their tongue is deceitful in their mouth.

VOICES [*offstage*]:   Boo! etc.

JEZEBEL: Jonah! Stop him!

MIRIAM: He's giving it all away.

AZARIAH: He'll have the Assyrians down on us in a week.

JONAH: Let them. That's what God wants—

MICAH: Therefore will I make thee desolate because of thy sins—Thou shalt sow, but thou shalt not reap— [*The* CROWD *is getting out of hand; boos and groans fill the offstage air.*] For the transgression of Jacob is all this, and for the sins of the house of Israel . . .

[*The* CROWD *is too noisy for him to be heard. He tries to quiet them with upraised hand.* JONAH, *who has been listening with growing dismay, slowly rises.*]

AZARIAH: Jonah! He's frightening them!

[*There is no help for it.* JONAH *moves fatefully toward the terrace, on the opposite side from* MICAH; *and holds up his hand. The* CROWD *turns silent, seeing him.*]

JONAH [*in a voice of despair*]:   I had a dream. And in the dream I rode upon the winds of heaven; upon the living breath of the Most High. Around me sounded the trumpets of the Host; and before me, in shining armor, rode the King of Israel—Pekah, Son of Remahliah, son of Jehosah, son of David. And the kings of Assyria and Damascus were troubled, and their thrones were moved; and darkness was upon Egypt. And a Voice said to me, Lo, this is Israel which is my daughter and my son and also my people, and I will stretch out my hand over them. And I will instruct Pekah the king . . . in all things . . . concerning my people . . .

[*The* CROWD *goes wild with joy.* AZARIAH *smiles with satisfaction;* JEZEBEL *looks relieved and triumphant;* MIRIAM *is clapping her hands.* JONAH *turns, and comes*

slowly back into the room . . . the picture of failure.
MICAH, *with folded arms, watches him somberly. Only*
JUDITH *regards him with pity, as—*

THE CURTAIN FALLS

ACT II

SCENE I

Evening. The same; a week later.

As the curtain rises, JEZEBEL *is reclining on the couch. She is partially nude, wrapped in a towel, and is holding up her leg for her own critical inspection. Beside the couch is a tray of oils and unguents.* MABELE, *in a large white apron, is busy lighting the lamps—such lamps of oil and tallow as used to decorate the palaces of Israel in the Eighth Century. The hills of Gad beyond the terrace, are dim and mysterious; night rises like a storm behind them. The lamplight is warm and yellow in the dusk.*

Having lighted the lamps, MABELE *returns to the couch prepared to massage her mistress with oils and unguents.*

MABELE: You want the Clover? Or the orange blossom?
JEZEBEL [*dreamily; admiring her leg*]:   Not bad, for a
    woman of my age . . . Oh—the orange blossom, I
    guess. The clover makes me smell like a farmer's
    daughter. A woman of my age—and antecedents.

65

MABELE [*at work*]: What's that?—Antecedents?

JEZEBEL: It's what you were. Like being a farmer's daughter.

MABELE: Want to hold your arm up just a little higher, milady?

JEZEBEL [*lazily reproving her*]: Your Highness.

MABELE: That's right—Your Highness. There hasn't been any news from Nineveh, has there—since Mr. Jonah made his speech—

JEZEBEL: No news. Just—peace.

MABELE: You think no news from Nineveh is good news? . . . It's mighty suspicious if you ask me. Those people—it's mostly when they're not doing anything, you can't tell *what* they're doing. Roll over, milady.

JEZEBEL [*vexed*]: Highness.

MABELE [*sulkily*]: Your Highness . . . Go on—roll over.

JEZEBEL [*turning, onto her stomach, and instructing* MABELE]: The Princess of Sharon. Of and From.

MABELE: Yes milady. What's that Of and From.

JEZEBEL: It's a kind of double title. It means that you belong to it—and it belongs to you. It's the highest nobility there is.

MABELE: Isn't that something? . . . You sure got knots in your shoulder—

JEZEBEL [*grunting*]: Ouch! Not so hard . . .

MABELE [*in reaction, her hands fly up toward her face; she sniffs at them curiously*]: *That's* what Mr. Jonah's been putting in his hair!

66

JEZEBEL: In his hair?

MABELE: Yes ma'am. He's just as flowery as an oleander tonight . . . You can smell him a mile away. I never did see him strut like that before. It's a wonder she wouldn't stay home sometimes, and leave us alone.

JEZEBEL: She's an old—friend.

MABELE: She's been here nearly every day. Mr. Jonah—

JEZEBEL: Prince Jonah.

MABELE: Yes milady. Prince Jonah. He sure has got himself up tonight. I figure he's got something on his mind.

JEZEBEL: You think so?

MABELE [*soberly*]:   Yes milady.

JEZEBEL: I think so, too, Mabele.

MABELE: And you don't mind?

JEZEBEL: Of course I mind. What do you think I am? Rub my back again, will you? Between the shoulders. [*as* MABELE *massages her*] I suppose what I mind isn't so much his doing . . . whatever it is he's doing. . . . What I mind most is his doing it to me. After all, my husband and I aren't lovers any more. I wouldn't care, so long as *I* was the one told him to go . . . or went myself.

MABELE [*shocked*]:   You'd leave him, Miss Jezebel?

JEZEBEL [*slowly*]:   No—I don't suppose I would. Twenty years are twenty years . . . you get used to things. But it's a mean world, Mabele. And I don't think I'd like . . . being alone in it . . .

[*She suddenly puts her head down to hide a tear.*]

67

MABELE: You crying, Miss Jezebel?

JEZEBEL [*fiercely*]:   Why the hell shouldn't I cry if I feel like it?

MABELE: Go ahead, go ahead . . . You've got a right not to be happy about that man.

JEZEBEL [*sitting up*]:   That man? I'm not happy about growing old! Hand me my mirror. [MABELE *hands her a long-handled mirror, in which* JEZEBEL *studies her face.*] You wouldn't think I was a beauty once, would you. Well—I was. A lot of men wanted me. All I had was my looks . . . and the dream of what I wanted . . . to have, and to be . . . Strange—what the years do to you . . . so little-by-little that it's hard to see the difference. One day you're sitting in the sunlight, warm and rosy . . . and all of a sudden, there's a little cloud over the sun. And you look up—and the sun is gone—and the warmth has gone out of the air . . . and it's time for the autumn rains. And you go home and look at yourself in the mirror—and there it is: the little veins you never saw before—the sag under the chin—the lost curve of the breast that no April will ever bring back again . . . and what have you got for your life? [*she looks around the room*] I could keep this palace . . . no—on second thought, I'd sell it, and just keep Sharon. A thousand acres. Four hundred, anyway. I could raise fruit. [*crying a little*] The hell with him!

MABELE: Tst, tst, tst. Ain't men something! [ASA *enters*

from R.; she turns on him in a fury] What you want,
you scoundrel?

ASA [*startled*]:   What you mean, scoundrel? What have
I done?

MABELE [*inexorably*]:   You were born, weren't you?

ASA: I had no pleasure from that. [*to* JEZEBEL] The
cook wants to know if Her Highness would take a look
at the carp's innards before she cooks it. She says it
looks like there might be an omen in it.

JEZEBEL [*eagerly*]:   An omen? Good or bad?

ASA: She didn't say, ma'am.

JEZEBEL [*getting up and wrapping towel around her*]:
We'd better have a look at it . . . where's your
master?

ASA: He's in the garden somewhere.

JEZEBEL: Go find him and tell him . . . [*on second
thought*] No—he doesn't believe in those things. Well
—maybe we'll be able to figure it out ourselves.

ASA: Yes, Your Highness.

JEZEBEL: Come, Mabele.

MABELE: Yes milady.

JEZEBEL [*irritated*]:   *He* can remember, why can't
you?

[*They go out.*]

[*The stage is empty for a moment. Then* JONAH *comes
in from L. He is dressed in his best—and most elegant—
coat; he wears a golden chain and a ring; and he carries
a vase of flowers, which he sets on the table. He steps*

69

back to study the effect; he hums tunelessly to himself.
He is quite a happy man. He looks at himself in JEZEBEL'S
mirror—puts his hand to his hair, then sniffs with satis-
faction. He rearranges his clothes; he goes to the terrace,
and looks out. Then he comes back in, and claps his
hands twice, sharply. When nothing happens, he tries
it again. ASA *appears R.*]

ASA: You want something, Mr. Jonah?

JONAH [*slightly aggrieved*]:   I clapped for you. Twice.

ASA [*wondering*]:   Why you clap for me instead of hol-
      lering?

JONAH: We're high up people now, Asa. My wife says
      Clap.

ASA [*with resignation*]:   Yes sir. What can I do for your
      Highness?

JONAH [*not quite certain why he clapped for Asa any-
      way*]:   How does the room look?

ASA [*noticing, now, the vase of flowers*]:   It looks all
      right—

JONAH [*turning around in front of him*]:   How do I
      look?

ASA [*admiring*]:   Oh my. [*taking a deep sniff, as* JONAH
      passes near him] Hmm-mm! You've outdone yourself
      tonight!

JONAH: Thank you. [*as though the idea had just oc-
      curred to him*] Asa—how would you like to go to the
      desert with me?

ASA [*cautiously*]:   What desert would that be, Mr.
      Jonah?

70

JONAH: Golan—

ASA [*shaking his head*]: No sir. I like it here.

JONAH: You'd be free there, practically. You'd be a free man!

ASA [*without enthusiasm*]: That's kindly meant, I'm sure.

JONAH [*surprised—and a little vexed*]: Don't you want to be free?

ASA: It isn't *are* you free—it's *where* you're free at. I could be free in my own country, if I was there. But I couldn't be free in the desert, Mr. Jonah. I'd have my lonesome fears.

JONAH: We all have our lonesome fears.

ASA: Yes sir. It's just that some have them lonesomer than others. Is there anything else now?

JONAH: No—that's all. If I want you, I'll . . . [*he looks at his hands*] I'll holler.

ASA: Yes sir.

[*He goes out, L. JONAH gazes after him thoughtfully; then slowly crosses the room. As he passes the portico, JUDITH appears on the terrace, a scarf over her hair. Evening has deepened.*]

JUDITH: Good evening, Jonah.

JONAH [*wheeling, caught by surprise*]: Well! There you are! [*he holds his hand out to her, she takes it, and comes down into the room*] How lovely you look. No—[*as she starts to take off her scarf*] Don't take it off. Let me see you . . . [*smiling*] half-hidden—like a girl's shy thoughts—

JUDITH [*confused, but pleased*]:   Really, Johnny! Such nonsense. At our age!

JONAH [*gallantly*]:   And what's the matter with our age, my dear? We've a good twenty years ahead of us.

JUDITH [*laughing ruefully*]:   Oh! [*she takes off her scarf and seats herself on the bench*] Now you've *really* spoiled my day! . . . It *is* our last evening, Johnny. Tomorrow I'll be on my way to Golan. Come—sit down; and tell me what you did all day. Begin with this morning.

JONAH [*sitting beside her*]:   Well . . . I woke up. And the sun was shining low and golden, and the birds were flying in and out of the olive tree outside my window.

JUDITH: They were having their breakfast.

JONAH: They were. They were very pleased with the whole thing.

JUDITH: And what did you do then?

JONAH: I thought about you.

JUDITH: Good. What did you think about me? Was it nice?

JONAH [*quietly*]:   I thought . . . that I loved you.

[JUDITH *sits very still. She looks away, touched and troubled.*]

JUDITH [*faintly*]:   Oh Johnny!

JONAH: Yes, it was nice. And I wondered if you were awake.

JUDITH [*low*]:   I thought my heart was dead—and now it's having breakfast in the olive trees.

72

JONAH: Greedy little creature.

JUDITH [*low*]:   I love you, too.

JONAH [*it is* JONAH's *turn to sit very still*]:   Do you?

[*He puts his hand on bench looking at her. She laces her fingers in his.*]

JUDITH [*sighs*]:   It's strange, isn't it . . . all those years you were living your life and I was living mine. Miles and miles apart. And probably never even thinking about each other.

JONAH: I did—about you.

JUDITH [*gaily*]:   Don't fib, Johnny. You didn't either.

JONAH: Well, I did. Sometimes.

JUDITH: Oh—sometimes. I did too—sometimes. But mostly, I just went about living—the way you do. From Monday to Tuesday, from Tuesday to Wednesday, from Wednesday to Thursday . . . If I'd only known!

JONAH: It was meant to be like this. Or you never would have come back to me.

[*There is a pause. She looks troubled.*]

JUDITH: Jonah—

JONAH: Yes, Judith.

JUDITH: Don't look at me. [*she turns his head away*] Just listen to me very closely and try to forgive me. I've a confession to make. I came here—hoping this would happen.

JONAH: That's no confession. I knew it all the time.

JUDITH: How did you know?

73

JONAH [*still not looking at her*]:   It took you so long to tell me about your three children.

JUDITH [*since she is being honest*]:   Four.

JONAH [*corrected*]:   Four. [*startled*] Four?

JUDITH: Hush . . . It doesn't matter. What matters is all those years . . . I worried about you.

JONAH [*surprised—but not unnaturally pleased*]:   About *me?*

JUDITH: You were the only true and honest person I had ever known . . . except old Nana, perhaps. And I was afraid that maybe you had changed—because of me . . . That you had grown proud, and hard . . . proud of your success . . . that the memory that we had together might have changed, too . . . for you. You see—it never changed . . . for me. A girl wants to think that what was lovely long ago really *was* lovely . . . that it never altogether lost its loveliness . . . But now I can go back to Golan and to my children with a peaceful heart. Because you're still the person I knew . . . and because what we had still has that memory of morning light . . .

JONAH: Darling—it isn't just a memory—

JUDITH [*a little sadly*]:   We can never really go back, Johnny.

JONAH: Why not?

JUDITH [*weakly—she isn't sure herself*]:   Why not?

JONAH [*urgently*]:   If you want it enough—

JUDITH [*more weakly still*]:   But . . . Jezebel . . . ?

74

JONAH: It had to come some day, Judy—for Jezebel and me. We should have separated long ago.

JUDITH: It's too late now—

JONAH: It's not too late. I've earned my life, darling. I have a right to my own happiness. After all, Jezebel is provided for; she has what she always wanted, a title and land. You should have been my wife, Judy, long ago. Be with me now.

JUDITH: Johnny—

JONAH [*urgently*]: For these last few years that are left us. For the last small hours of the evening.

JUDITH: No, Johnny—don't—you mustn't.

JONAH: We'll start all over again from where we were long ago.

[*He kisses her.*]

JUDITH [*tearing herself away finally*]: If anyone saw us!

JONAH: Let them!

JUDITH [*rearranging her hair*]: I must look a sight . . . Darling—be sensible!

JONAH: Not now!

JUDITH: Behave yourself!

JONAH: I don't want to.

JUDITH: At least—till we're alone together!

JONAH [*elated*]: Judith!

JUDITH: Oh Johnny—is it really possible?

[*They embrace.*]

JONAH: It had to be!

JUDITH: But—what will we *do*?

75

JONAH: We'll go away together. We'll leave all this—
We'll travel. We'll—we'll go somewhere. To Egypt . . .

JUDITH: Won't it be hot in Egypt, darling? Now?

JONAH: To Abyssinia . . . No, that will be even hotter.

JUDITH: Couldn't we go to some lovely island in the sea?

JONAH: Not in the sea, dear—

JUDITH: Johnny—Are you sure this is the right thing for you?

JONAH [*simply*]:   What is? Having you?

JUDITH: No—that doesn't trouble me. I mean . . . leaving all this—

JONAH [*carelessly*]:   This? It belongs to Jezebel, anyway. I'll have twice this, some day.

JUDITH [*startled*]:   Twice . . . this?

JONAH [*smiling*]:   Judy—Do you know how many sightseers there were in the palace this morning? Over three hundred!

JUDITH [*uncertainly*]:   Well—that's very nice, dear—but . . .

JONAH: I had to sign autographs. That's never happened before. You see—a prophet is only as good as his last prophecy—

JUDITH: But I thought you wanted to give up prophecy!

JONAH: They won't let me. Look: the Veterans of our Foreign Wars sent me this gold chain.

JUDITH [*gravely*]:   Do you mean because of that dream, darling?

JONAH: The King sent me this ring. It's very substantial.

JUDITH [*inspecting it*]:   It's very pretty.

JONAH: It's an emerald.

JUDITH: Yes. I see.

JONAH [*almost too carelessly*]:   They made me a Prince, you know—

JUDITH [*low*]:   You told me.

JONAH: I've come a long way, Judy. A long way. They say I'm even greater than Ezekiel.

JUDITH: That does mean a lot to you, doesn't it—

JONAH: I thought I might do some preaching next season. They've asked for me in Beth Arbea and in Hebron. I might even go to Gilead and Sharon—they always loved me in Gilead.

JUDITH: But darling—this isn't what I thought. I mean . . . I don't know if I'm right for this . . .

JONAH: You'll soon be used to it.

JUDITH: Oh, no, dear.

JONAH: After all, Judy—it's all for you . . .

JUDITH: But Jonah dear—it mustn't be for me. It can't be for me. I wouldn't know how to be a person like that.

JONAH: Like what?

JUDITH: Like . . . I've got to think a little.

JONAH: Judy—what's wrong? What's happened?

JUDITH [*slowly*]:   I don't know. Only—everything is different, somehow . . . It isn't the way—it used to be— . . . Perhaps that's my fault; perhaps I shouldn't have expected it. I want to think, Johnny—I've got to

77

think. I've lost us somewhere . . . I'm going out on the terrace for a while . . . don't come with me; I want to be by myself.

JONAH [*miserably*]:   Judy—what have I said? Only that I'm happy—and that I love you.

JUDITH [*gently*]:   I know. Don't worry. I wouldn't want you to be unhappy, ever. Not for anything. Not even with me. [*she bends and kisses him gently*] I've got to find us again, that's all. If I can.

[*She goes out swiftly, C.*]

JONAH [*picking up her scarf*]:   You forgot your scarf . . . [*He gets to his feet and holds it out to her—but she has gone. He smiles, a little uncertainly; it is blue evening now, and growing dark. He turns the scarf over in his hand; and for a moment puts it to his face. Then, still holding it, he sighs, and straightens up; and turning toward the doorway, R., calls out*] Oh—Jezebel—

[*And starts across the stage, to try to find her. He hasn't too far to go; before he gets to the doorway,* JEZEBEL *herself comes through it, still wrapped in her towel.*]

JEZEBEL [*coolly*]:   Hi.

JONAH: Oh! Hello. I was just coming to find you.

JEZEBEL: I was in the kitchen. Looking at the fish.

JONAH: Fish? What fish?

JEZEBEL: Trying to figure out what an eel in a carp's stomach, with a frog in its mouth means.

JONAH: An eel? In *our* carp's stomach?

JEZEBEL: With a frog in its mouth.

JONAH [*suddenly apprehensive*]: It means *some-thing* . . .

JEZEBEL: That's what the cook thought.

JONAH [*worried and thoughtful*]: There's a meaning *somewhere* . . . there has to be. A frog, swallowed by a . . . [*he gives a start*] Nineveh!

JEZEBEL: What do you mean—Nineveh?

JONAH [*he is quite sure he's right*]: Like me . . . swallowed by a whale . . . don't you see?

JEZEBEL: But this is an eel.

JONAH: It's symbolic.

JEZEBEL: Is it good for the Jews?

JONAH [*doubtfully*]: It was good once . . .

JEZEBEL: Well—make up your mind. What's that you're hiding behind you?

[JONAH *somewhat sheepishly brings the scarf out from behind his back.*]

JONAH: I sort of wanted to talk to you about something.

JEZEBEL [*quickly*]: Really—a prophet who can't tell what a simple thing like a frog . . .

JONAH [*insistent*]: Jezebel! I want to talk to you.

JEZEBEL [*fiercely*]: An omen if I ever saw one.

JONAH: Jezebel . . . I've got to tell you . . .

JEZEBEL: Jonah, I don't want to hear it! Whatever it is, I don't want to hear it. Not in— [*she looks down at her bath towel*] not without clothes on.

JONAH [*stupidly*]: What's that got to do with it?

JEZEBEL [*desperately*]: Look—Do what you like. Just don't—tell me about it.

79

JONAH: It's simply that . . . that—

[VOICES *are heard off*—AZARIAH's *and* ASA's *in contrapuntal hubbub.*]

ASA'S VOICE: Mr. Jonah!

AZARIAH'S VOICE: Jonah! Jezebel!

ASA'S VOICE: Mr. Jonah! Mr. Jonah! Lean on me, Councillor—lean on me.

[AZARIAH *comes staggering in R., leaning on* ASA. *He is in armor, but dusty and disheveled, and short of breath. He staggers across the room, and collapses on the bench.* JONAH *and* JEZEBEL *stare at him open-mouthed.*]

AZARIAH: Oh my back! [*he sits down on a chair*] It's finished.

JEZEBEL: What's finished? What do you mean?

AZARIAH: The Kingdom. Us. [*realizing that neither* JONAH *nor* JEZEBEL *has heard the news*] Good God— don't you know? We're at war!

JONAH [*shocked*]: At war?

AZARIAH [*nods*]: Three days ago. Invaded—overrun. Without a word of warning.

JEZEBEL: Nineveh!

AZARIAH: Our army met the enemy yesterday, by the Sea of Cinnereth—Where the King was fishing with some of his ladies. We sustained an overwheming defeat.

[ASA *gives* AZARIAH *glass.*]

JONAH [*dully to* JEZEBEL]: It wasn't good—that eel.

AZARIAH: The army is in flight. I am a little ahead of it.

JEZEBEL: Oh—!

AZARIAH: The King left the battlefield early, with a handful of his captains. He asked me to take Miriam into my chariot . . . in the confusion I lost her. God knows where she is.

JEZEBEL: How awful!

AZARIAH: Tiglath has taken Ijon, and Kadesh—Maacah —all of Gilead—the Assyrian flag flies over Napthali.

JONAH [*stupidly*]: Then—they'll be here—

AZARIAH: Before another day is over.

[JONAH *involuntarily looks toward the terrace and the night beyond.*]

ASA: Lord! Lord!

JEZEBEL: Be quiet. [*to* AZARIAH] Is the road still open to the coast?

AZARIAH: I shouldn't be surprised.

JONAH [*almost to himself*]: Judith!

[JONAH *moves anxiously to the terrace. He looks to the right and left; he searches for* JUDITH. *She is not there.*]

AZARIAH: What was left of us headed in that direction. Tiglath's chariots will be coming from the North and from the East— Not for another ten hours.

[*He winces as he feels his back.*]

JEZEBEL [*musing*]: Have they taken Sharon?

AZARIAH: No—but they will.

[MIRIAM's *voice is heard off.*]

MIRIAM'S VOICE: Jezebel O Jezebel—

[MABELE *runs in, frightened, from R.*]

MABELE: Miss Jezebel—Miss Miriam's here . . . Looking awful! She's had an accident or something . . .

[ASA *goes to her, and puts his arms around her. She begins to whimper; at the same time,* MIRIAM *bursts in from R. She wears whatever the well-dressed Jewess would have worn in 731 B.C., when fishing with the King on the Sea of Cinnereth. But she is considerably mussed, and travel-stained; and her fine new bonnet is set awry on her head.*]

MIRIAM: All is lost! [*she sees* AZARIAH] Oh—*there* you are—you louse!

AZARIAH [*plaintively*]:   Where were you?

MIRIAM [*indignantly*]:   Where was I? I was a hundred yards ahead of you, rounding the Sea of Cinnereth— and a mile behind you at Beth Arbea. I wouldn't be here at all—except that I managed to catch a ride in a supply chariot as far as Rimmon! [*to* JEZEBEL] My dear—I'm pooped. In and out of ditches all day long — I'm not up to that kind of nonsense any more.

[*She makes for the couch.*]

MABELE [*wailing*]:   O-oh, Miss Jezebel!

JEZEBEL: Hush, Mabele . . . Nothing's going to happen to you . . . for the moment, anyway. [*to* MIRIAM, *as she leads her toward the couch, eases her down onto it*] The question is—what are we going to do. You say we can still get out—?

MIRIAM: One jump ahead of the whole Assyrian army!

AZARIAH: From the coast one could get south—by ship—

MIRIAM: I've got an aunt with a little place near the Red Sea—

JEZEBEL: That's all very well—but what about me?

MIRIAM: What do you mean, Jez—what about you?

JEZEBEL: I have no friends in the South—

AZARIAH [*uncomfortably*]:   You'll manage some way.

JEZEBEL [*fiercely*]:   How? On someone's charity? I've
been too great for that. This is my home . . . I've
lived in it—a long while. Twenty years, almost. I've
had what I wanted in the world . . . : Well—that's
over now. But to be a fugitive besides . . . without
dignity . . . No. Life isn't that sweet. Not to me.

[*No one says anything for a moment.* MIRIAM *has picked
up* JEZEBEL's *mirror, and is looking at herself in it. She
tries—in vain—to straighten her hat.*]

MIRIAM: I look a sight.

AZARIAH: At the moment I don't believe I could move
another step. [*to* JEZEBEL] I think at earliest daylight—
if I'm not putting you out—?

[JEZEBEL *turns to* MIRIAM.]

MIRIAM [*realizing that* JEZEBEL *is waiting for her to say
something*]:   Eh? Oh . . . I don't care what we do. I
want a bath. Tiglath can't do any worse to me than
those last five miles.

JEZEBEL [*purposefully*]:   That's that, then. Asa, you go
tell the cook to put another fish on the fire. And never
mind the auguries this time. Prince Azariah and Miss
Miriam are staying the night. As for me—I'm going up
to dress.

MABELE [*wailing*]:   We're not going to stay here, are
we? And let those Assyrians do the things they do?

83

JEZEBEL: Whatever it is they do, I don't intend to do it
in a bath towel. Azariah, you'll find a basin and some
warm water in Jonah's room. Make yourself comfortable. Mabele, suppose you go ahead, and fix a hot bath
for Miss Miriam. Put a few rose petals in it; she likes
them. Asa—help the Councillor . . . Run along, Mabele—

MABELE: Yes, ma'am.

[*She goes tearfully out L. ASA goes to give AZARIAH his
arm.*]

MIRIAM [*rising cheerfully*]:   Thank you, dear; you're
very thoughtful. I always say there's nothing like a
nice hot tub after a long day in the country. [*she
crosses to the doorway, L. and stops a moment*] By the
way—I saw your friend, Mrs. Hiram, down the road.
She was in an awful hurry. She was crying. What has
she got to cry about? She's probably halfway to the
coast by now. If she got a ride.

[*She goes out U.L.*]

JEZEBEL [*thoughtfully*]:   So!

[*JONAH comes in from the terrace, from a fruitless search
for JUDITH. He and JEZEBEL look at each other quietly.*]

JEZEBEL: Your friend has left.

JONAH: I know.

JEZEBEL: The road to the coast is still open. Take it if
you like. It's of no interest to me.

[*She goes up the stairs. JONAH looks after her; he looks
at the scarf in his hand, and at the night outside. He is
miserable; bewildered, and heartsick. ASA enters, R.*]

ASA: Can I do anything for you, Mr. Jonah?

JONAH: You'd better leave, Asa, while you can. You and Mabele.

ASA: Yes sir.

JONAH: You're free—both of you. The road is still open. Goodbye,—and—God bless you.

ASA: Yes sir. Are you leaving?

JONAH: I'm not going anywhere.

ASA: It's a long way to freedom, Mr. Jonah; I don't know as we would care to make the journey alone. Will you be having dinner with the others?

JONAH: Dinner . . . ? You know, I always rather liked this view. We ought to be able to see the Assyrian torches from here, before too long. I think I'll just stay here a while and wait. Put out the lights, Asa . . . I'm going to sit, and watch the night . . .

[*He seats himself on the rim of the portico.* ASA *puts out the lights; the scene darkens;* JONAH *is left silhouetted against the night sky.*]

JONAH: You—out there beyond the evening, and the morning star—are You satisfied, now that You have sent the wind to wither me again? Look—I am not vain any longer. If only You had been more patient with me . . . or spoken to me . . . If only You had spoken to me! They loved me in Gilead; I would have told them about You. Because I loved You . . . Or have You gone so far away that it no longer matters to You? But it *must* matter, Lord, what happens to a man! We are Your witness here; through us You see the

light of earth, with us You walk upon the hills . . .
because of us . . . however unworthy. . . . There is
no answer; there is no reply. In the morning the horns
of Assyria will answer me. I shall wait for them.

CURTAIN

SCENE II

_____

*The same, early next morning. In the cold, misty dawn-
light,* JONAH *is discovered asleep, wrapped in a blanket,
and propped against a pillar of the portico. The distant
horns of the Assyrians are heard from the valley. The
shadowy figure of a man, muffled in a long cloak, appears
on the terrace, and stealthily approaches the portico—
only to freeze in surprise as he sees* JONAH. JONAH *stirs,
stretches, and yawns; he sits up and stiffens in alarm at
the sight of the hooded figure before him. His alarm turns
to astonishment as the man uncovers his face.*

JONAH: Micah!
MICAH: Sh!
JONAH: What are you doing here?
MICAH [*still in a hoarse whisper*]:   Are you all right?
JONAH: Of course I'm all right. Why shouldn't I be?
MICAH [*mysteriously*]:   Are they—here?

JONAH: Are who here?

MICAH [*coming in, but looking around furtively*]:   The Assyrians—

JONAH [*cheerfully*]:   Oh. No—not yet.

MICAH [*hoarsely*]:   Then there's still time—

JONAH: Time? For what?

MICAH: To get you out of here.

JONAH [*surprised and touched*]:   My dear boy! That's very kind of you. But if I'd wanted to get out, I could have left last night.

MICAH: And you didn't?

JONAH: Obviously not—none of us did.

MICAH: Then you're all here!

JONAH: All . . . except one.

MICAH: That's bad.

JONAH: Come in, my boy, come in . . . it's cold out there. Why should you care what happens to me, Micah?

MICAH [*holding out a large, brown feather*]:   An angel dropped this on me.

JONAH [*takes it, inspects it dubiously*]:   Looks like a hawk to me.

MICAH [*stubbornly*]:   It's too big for a hawk.

JONAH: And it's too small for an angel.

MICAH: Not for a small angel.

JONAH: It's a hawk. Possibly a vulture.

MICAH: Why would a vulture wake me up and say, "Micah"?

JONAH: When did you eat last?

87

MICAH: Two days ago.

JONAH: Did you see a fox, too? And did he ask you whether God had a tail?

MICAH: Don't confuse me! You've confused me enough! After that speech of yours about the dream, I went back to the desert. I kept thinking to myself, why did he do it? Because it wasn't true . . . was it?

JONAH [*low*]:   No . . . it wasn't true.

MICAH: Then why?

JONAH: I didn't want to. I wasn't going to. And then you started to frighten people—and I had to comfort them.

MICAH [*startled*]:   You want to *comfort* people?

JONAH [*simply*]:   I've—comforted them all my life, I guess.

MICAH: That's what bothers me. I thought and thought about it. How you told people that God loved them— and I told them He didn't. And I was right, and you were wrong . . . and yet—nobody liked me.

JONAH: Did you expect them to?

MICAH: Everybody liked you. And—God loves you, Jonah. Why, I don't know.

JONAH: God loves me? No—Not God.

MICAH [*extending the feather again*]:   My angel told me to find you and bring you back to the desert again.

JONAH: Thank you. That's very good of him. But I don't think so, Micah. There was a time when I thought— I could go back—as I was; but I was wrong. So—since I seem to have come to the end—why not wait for it—

quietly? Sometimes I think that death isn't half the
enemy that life is. It's a hawk's feather, Micah.

[JEZEBEL *comes down the steps briskly, from L. Rear.
She looks very neat and efficient.*]

JEZEBEL: Hello, Micah—what are you doing here? I
thought you were safe in the desert.

JONAH: He came—to take us out, my dear.

JEZEBEL: Oh? That was sweet of you, Micah. But we're
staying.

MICAH: I know.

JONAH: That's no reason for *you* to be caught. You
young men must look to the future.

MICAH: What future is there? Wars, and rumors of
war—

JEZEBEL [*cheerfully*]:   It's not very appetizing, is it?
. . . Have you had breakfast?

MICAH: I'm not hungry, thank you.

JEZEBEL: You'd better eat something, while you can. Assyrian food may not agree with you. Go find Mabele,
and tell her there'll be one extra for breakfast. You'll
find her in there— [*she motions L.*] somewhere—

MICAH [*to* JONAH]:   You won't leave, Jonah?

JONAH: No.

[MICAH *goes out L.*]

JEZEBEL [*to* JONAH]:   Did you go to bed at all last night?

JONAH: No.

JEZEBEL: You look it. You could at least have tried to
get some sleep.

JONAH: I did sleep a little. The horns woke me.

JEZEBEL: They woke me, too. They must be fairly near.

JONAH: I hope the others get off all right—

JEZEBEL: They should be awake by now . . . [*almost too carelessly*] What will happen to—all this, do you think?

JONAH [*calmly*]:   They'll burn it, I suppose.

JEZEBEL: Burn it! . . . How can you sit there . . . ?

JONAH [*reasonably*]:   What else should I do?

JEZEBEL: You and your prophecies!

JONAH [*surprised*]:   What?

JEZEBEL: Telling people that God was with us! Why—you yourself said He'd gone to heaven-knows-where.

JONAH: You were rather pleased with me a week ago—

JEZEBEL: So now it's *my* fault! What a wretched little creature you are, Jonah!

JONAH [*gently*]:   I never said it was your fault, Jezebel. You were always pleased with me when things went well. And you were right—for you. The trouble is—*I* was pleased, too. And that was wrong. It's not a prophet's business to be pleased.

JEZEBEL [*scornfully*]:   I suppose you'd have been better off in a cave!

JONAH: That was my failure. I hated caves.

JEZEBEL: Try not to be a hypocrite, Jonah.

JONAH: I know, I know. I'm trying not to be. The trouble is—I haven't much time left to be honest in. Neither have you.

JEZEBEL [*proudly*]:   At least—*I* don't regret what I had. I'd do it again—if I could.

JONAH: I'm afraid I never knew what I had . . . until it wasn't there any more. Until I had turned my back on it—and lost it. It wasn't God who went to heaven knows where . . . it was me. I. Years ago.

JEZEBEL [*slowly*]:   I see. You blame me for everything, don't you?

JONAH [*with painful humor*]:   On the contrary—I blame the whale—for throwing me up again.

[AZARIAH *enters hurriedly from the terrace.*]

AZARIAH: Who's up? Oh—you? Where's Miriam? The chariot's all ready—ready to go—[*Assyrian horns are heard:* AZARIAH *listens intensely*] They're still a good hour away . . . [*to* JEZEBEL] I've got room for you, if you've changed your mind—

JEZEBEL: I haven't.

AZARIAH: Jonah?

JONAH: No. But you can take Micah.

AZARIAH: That hoodlum? No thank you! What's *he* doing here?

JONAH: Having breakfast.

AZARIAH [*indignantly*]:   Breakfast! At a time like this? The man is mad.

JONAH [*firmly*]:   Take him with you, Azariah.

AZARIAH: Agh! [*but he gives in*] All right. Where's Miriam?

JEZEBEL: She's not up yet.

AZARIAH [*nearly apoplectic*]:   Not up yet!? Why—we—ought to be on the road already—

[MIRIAM *comes sleepily down the steps from L. She is dressed in one of* JEZEBEL's *gowns.*]

MIRIAM [*yawning*]:   Ooooh. What time is it? Those damn horns woke me—

AZARIAH: Miriam! Let's get going.

MIRIAM: All right—all right . . . mmm! That big soft, roomy bed . . . all to myself.

JEZEBEL: Do you want some breakfast, darling?

AZARIAH: For heaven's sake, Jezebel—we've no time—

MIRIAM: Well, I wish you were going with us, Jez. Are you sure you won't change your mind? [JEZEBEL *shakes her head*] Well, goodbye, dear. And if I don't see you again—

[*Kisses* JEZEBEL.]

AZARIAH [*impatiently*]:   Come along, Miriam.

JEZEBEL: That's a lovely outfit, dear. Have I seen it before?

MIRIAM: It's one of yours.

JEZEBEL: Of course—

MIRIAM: I didn't think you'd mind.

AZARIAH: For God's sake, Miriam. [*looks at* JONAH] Women! Even on Judgment Day!

[JONAH *chuckles.*]

MIRIAM: All right—all right! Goodbye, Jez, and good luck.

AZARIAH: Goodbye, Jezebel . . . Jonah.

MIRIAM: 'Bye, Jonah.

JONAH [*suddenly*]:   Don't forget Micah.

AZARIAH: I'll drive out past the front of the palace. Send
  him down.

MIRIAM [*as an afterthought*]:   Oh, Jez . . .

AZARIAH [*grabs* MIRIAM's *hand fiercely*]:   Come on!

[*He and* MIRIAM *hurry out onto the terrace. Suddenly
the Assyrian horns sound very close. They stop, shocked
at what they see.*]

MIRIAM: Oh—oh.

[*They come slowly in.* MIRIAM *quiet.* AZARIAH *drooping.*]

AZARIAH [*dully*]:   It's too late.

MIRIAM: We've got visitors.

AZARIAH: Trapped. Like a pig.

MIRIAM [*with an attempt at lightness*]:   Well, it's been
  nice knowing you all. [*regretfully*] We could have had
  breakfast, too.

[AZARIAH *tries to control the trembling of his limbs.*
MIRIAM *takes a slightly sardonic view of the proceedings;*
JEZEBEL *draws herself up;* JONAH *seems almost indif-
ferent.*]

[*An* ASSYRIAN COLONEL *enters, followed by two Assyrian
soldiers. He is dressed in full armor; He clicks his heels,
and salutes.* MIRIAM *straightens her hat.*

COLONEL: Lord Jonah?

JONAH: Yes—?

COLONEL: Colonel Harubabel here. From His Imperial
  Majesty Tiglath Pileser, King of Assyria and Nineveh,
  Emperor of Babylonia, of Elam, of Mesopotamia, Ty-
  rant of Accad, of Sus, Divine Consort of Astarte, Lion

of Chaldee, Bull of Bulls, Son of the Sun, and Friend
of the Poor—greetings.

JONAH [*respectful, but dignified*]:   Yes?

COLONEL: The Light of Asia will enter this room, ac-
companied by the usual flourishes in just [*he glances
at a sun dial in his hand, and at the sunlight outside*]
thirty seconds. He suggests that you prepare yourselves
by assuming positions of relative relaxation . . . since
you will naturally be standing for some time. Any questions?

AZARIAH: Are—are you going to kill us?

COLONEL [*impassively*]:   I believe it is customary. [SOL-
DIERS *now appear on the terrace; there is a flourish of
trumpets, and* TIGLATH PILESER *mounts the terrace, and
strides down into the hall*] His Imperial Majesty,
Tiglath Pileser, King of Assyria and Nineveh, Emperor
of Babylonia, of Elam, of Mesopotamia . . .

TIGLATH: Enough. Enough. [*the* KING OF NINEVEH *is a
bearded, regal figure, in the Assyrian manner—fierce
and hawklike, but no fool, and no barbarian. Behind
him, indignant and disheveled, held fast by two soldiers, comes* REBECCA] Does anybody here know this
woman? [*he motions to* REBECCA] She claims to be a
friend of yours.

MIRIAM: Becky!

TIGLATH: Then you do know her? [*to the* SOLDIERS] Let
her go. [REBECCA *is pushed forward into the room, and
stumbles over to the couch, where she sinks down
damp and tearful.* MIRIAM *goes over to comfort her*]

94

We picked her up back of our lines—with a sling-shot in her hands.

REBECCA [*tearful and indignant*]: It's all a lie about David and Goliath.

TIGLATH: What's the matter with you people? Are you trying to commit suicide? Where's the other one?

[TWO SOLDIERS *bring forward* JUDITH. *She is calm and composed.*]

JONAH: Judith!

JUDITH: Hello, Johnny.

TIGLATH: So you know her too, eh? All right—let her go.

JONAH [*to* JUDITH]: I thought *you* were safe, at least!

COLONEL: Silence, please.

TIGLATH [*to the* COLONEL]: Harubabel—Who is that?

COLONEL: That is Jonah, Your Majesty.

TIGLATH [*pleased*]: Ah! It is, eh? He looks a little younger than I expected. [*pointing to* JUDITH] Who is that, then? His wife?

JONAH: No, Your Majesty.

JEZEBEL: *I* am his wife, Sire.

TIGLATH [*glancing at her*]: Hm . . . I see. [*pointing to* MIRIAM] And that one?

JEZEBEL: The Lady Miriam, Your Majesty.

TIGLATH: It seems to me I've heard of her . . . [*to* AZARIAH] *Your* face looks familiar.

AZARIAH [*unhappily*]: I'm Azariah, Majesty. . . . Councillor to the late King Pekah—

TIGLATH [*surprised*]: The late? Why? Has he had an accident?

95

AZARIAH [*in confusion*]:   No . . . I don't know . . . I thought . . . naturally . . .

TIGLATH [*laughing*]:   Oh! That? Nonsense. The war is over—except for a few details. I don't want Pekah's hide . . . I have half his kingdom. By the Bull! He'll do me more good on his throne, as a buffer to the south. But no more lend-lease to Egypt! That's an order.

AZARIAH [*eagerly*]:   Yes, sir. Your Majesty . . . no indeed—I understand—

TIGLATH [*interrupting*]:   The man I want to talk to now, is Jonah. You, sir.

JONAH [*courteously*]:   Majesty?

TIGLATH [*musing*]:   Yes—you're younger than I thought. So you're the famous . . . Tell me—were you actually . . .

JONAH [*quickly*]:   Yes, Your Majesty—three days and three nights.

TIGLATH: It really happened then. I must say I expected something more venerable . . . almost classical. Still —you'll do, I guess. How would you like to come work for me?

JONAH [*startled*]:   For you?

TIGLATH [*testily*]:   For me. For Nineveh. What's the difference?

JONAH [*stammering*]:   None. But . . . I . . . I . . .

TIGLATH: I'm tired of sheep guts and giblets. Nineveh needs a prophet. I could make you a very good offer.

JONAH: But why me, Your Majesty?

TIGLATH: I want a man who can curl people's hair just by opening his mouth. Don't forget—it was you who put us into sackcloth and ashes that time. . . . My father never forgot it.

JONAH: You honor me, Sire—but—

TIGLATH: Let me finish. I've had this on my mind a long time, ever since I started reading the Psalms. I'm a simple man, but I have a great respect for literature. "The Lord is my shepherd; I shall not want." Most unlikely, of course—but what language! . . . I've got an idea that some day nations are going to be renowned not for what they do, but for what they say. The Word lives, when the wars are forgotten. That's why I want to rewrite our histories. Look at the Sumerians; they were lords of the earth, and of Chaldee—and whom do the people remember? Abraham. A lonely sheepherder. But he had the language of the prophets. By the Bull! I want a prophet, too!—How about it? Well?

[*They all murmur in wonder.*]

JONAH [*slowly*]: I am greatly complimented, Your Majesty.

JUDITH [*faintly*]: Johnny!

AZARIAH: Yes. Indeed—he'll be glad to!

MIRIAM: Certainly he will.

JEZEBEL: Of course he will! I think it's wonderful!

JONAH: Yes, I know you do.

TIGLATH [*with satisfaction*]: That's that, then.

JONAH: But Your Majesty—

TIGLATH [*sharply*]: There are no buts.

JONAH [*feebly*]:   But—

TIGLATH: The last man who said But to me is currently being digested by the ravens of three separate provinces.

[MICAH *appears in the doorway L.*]

MICAH: Breakfast's served.

[*After one astonished look, he ducks hastily back again.*]

TIGLATH: Who in the Name of the Bull was that?

JEZEBEL: That was Micah, Your Majesty—a young prophet from Golan.

TIGLATH [*heartily*]:   Good. We'll take him along with us —as a kind of spare wheel . . . Did he say breakfast?

JEZEBEL: Yes, Sire. [*timidly*] Would you . . . ?

TIGLATH: By all means! Ladies—gentlemen—I seem to have developed an appetite. Shall we go in? Come along, Harry—

[*Motioning to the* COLONEL *to follow, he strides off R. The others troop after him, not without trepidation—all except* JONAH *and* JUDITH. *At the doorway,* JEZEBEL *turns back toward them.*]

JEZEBEL [*sharply*]:   You coming, Jonah?

JONAH: In a moment—

JEZEBEL [*in command again*]:   Well—see that it *is* a moment, please. Don't start in by being rude; and don't do anything foolish. [*indicating* TIGLATH] He isn't playing, you know. Mrs. Hiram, I'll see that you're escorted wherever you want to go. You won't see my husband again, I'm afraid . . . This is a big thing for him. Quite a big thing. Say goodbye, Jonah, and come to breakfast. You might wear one of your decorations, I think. Goodbye, Mrs. Hiram . . . I keep forgetting; you *are* a princess, aren't you? Goodbye, Your Highness; I wish you every happiness.

JUDITH: Thank you, Lady Jezebel.

JEZEBEL: I'm a princess, too. Goodbye.

[JEZEBEL *goes out R.* JONAH *and* JUDITH *look at each other for a moment; then, with a cry,* JUDITH *rushes into* JONAH'S *arms.*]

JUDITH: Oh, Johnny!

JONAH: Well—you're safe, anyway . . .

JUDITH: I don't care—

JONAH: I couldn't believe my eyes.

JUDITH: I hadn't gotten very far. And there were soldiers everywhere—

JONAH: I thought you'd left me—

JUDITH: I *had* left you, darling. You see—I couldn't have gone with you . . . not with all that fame and glory. That wasn't the you I loved—that was someone else. I wouldn't have been happy—and neither would you.

JONAH: Well—it doesn't matter now, does it. I wonder . . . what your children would have made of me.

JUDITH: They would have liked the idea of having a father, I think.

JONAH [*wistfully*]:   Is it very hard to be a father?

JUDITH: Yes.

JONAH: That would frighten me.

99

JUDITH: You'd have done all right. You just have to be very forbidding—and very forgiving. Besides—they'd have been mothering you in a week!

JONAH: Tell me about them, darling.

JUDITH [*picking them off on her fingers*]:   Well, there's Huldah, my eldest. She's sixteen. Trying to do the impossible—to be like all the other sixteen-year-olds, and at the same time absolutely unique and irreplaceable . . . Don't you think you'd better go back in, darling?

JONAH [*quietly, but firmly*]:   There's time yet—Go on—

JUDITH: Then there's Abigail—she's fourteen, and very very emotional. She feels that no one understands her, and that her life is a failure. And Deborah at eleven—in love with the little boy down the road. He's the son of our local bandit, and he can spit through his teeth, and look very fierce . . . Johnny—the King . . . you mustn't keep him waiting . . .

JONAH [*inexorably*]:   Go on—

JUDITH: And then . . . There's Hepzibah; she's nine, and dances like an angel, [*she stops counting on her fingers*] and goes around in a lovely dream of herself. And Dido; she's the baby.

JONAH: That's five!

JUDITH [*innocently*]:   Is it? It is, isn't it.

JONAH [*severely*]:   Judy!

JUDITH [*humbly*]:   I know. I always think one ought to tell people things as gently as possible . . . [*she looks at him anxiously*] Does it make a difference, Johnny?

JONAH [*gently*]:   Nothing makes any difference any

more, I'm afraid. I learned a great deal, last night,
Judy—just from the silence. It's very good for the soul
—silence. I thought how impatient I used to be with
God—because He took His own time, and His own
way, of doing things. And all the time, I wanted to be
great . . . You never cared if I were great or not, did
you, Judy?

JUDITH: Only for what made you happy. What does it
matter *what* I wanted?

JONAH: Or I, either! I'm to be great, now, in Nineveh.
I am well served, Judy—for what I made of myself.

JUDITH [*weeping*]:   Oh Johnny, Johnny! I should have
gone with you—

JONAH [*gently*]:   No, my darling—you were right. I
learned that, too . . . A man must go by himself, in
silence—to seek God; as one goes down into the sea.
Perhaps, if I had gone to Him alone, He might have
spoken to me just once more. And then I could have
come back to you as I used to be—as you remembered
me—

JUDITH: I only remember that I love you, and that I
failed you. Nothing else matters.

JONAH: It does matter, Judy—even though the story is
over. A young man's love is like April—all rain and
blossom. But autumn needs God's remembrance . . .
for the autumn leaves.

MABELE [*offstage*]:   Mr. Jonah! Mr. Jonah!

[MABELE *comes rushing out of the dining hall L.*]

JONAH: —What's the matter here . . . ?

MABELE [*breathlessly*]:   Mr. Jonah—Mr. Jonah!

JONAH: Yes? What is it?

MABELE: Did you see what I saw? Or didn't I see it?

JONAH: What did you see, Mabele?

MABELE: That man! Sitting in there—looking the spitting image of Tiglath *Pi*leser. Eating our eggs—like they was his!

JONAH: It *is* Tiglath Pileser, Mabele. He's having breakfast.

MABELE: With Miss Jezebel?

JONAH: That's right.

MABELE: How come a thing like that can happen to decent people like us?

JONAH [*ruefully*]:   He wants us to go north with him, to Nineveh.

MABELE [*wide-eyed*]:   But Mr. Jonah—!

JONAH: There are no buts, Mabele.

MABELE: But—

JONAH: Do you want to be digested by the ravens of three separate provinces?

MABELE: Oh no sir. I wouldn't be able to reassemble myself in the hereafter.

JONAH [*with a shrug*]:   Well—there you are.

[TIGLATH, HARUBABEL, REBECCA *and* AZARIAH *come out of the dining hall, followed by* JEZEBEL *and* MIRIAM.]

TIGLATH [*with hearty concern*]:   What's the matter with the wench?

JONAH: She had a little fright, Your Majesty. She thought she saw you.

TIGLATH: Well—Tell her to hurry up and get you people packed. I want to be in Rimmon by noon.
Harubabel!

COLONEL: Yes, Sire—

[TIGLATH *goes up to speak to him,* MABELE *scuttles off
up the steps, L.* TIGLATH *turns back to* JONAH.]

TIGLATH [*heartily*]:   Yes, indeed—I always say, give me
the children until they're nine years old and you can
have them the rest of their lives. They'll die good Assyrians. Language—that's the thing to teach people
what's good for them . . . We'll get on, you and I.
Come along.

JONAH [*detaining him*]:   You honor me, Sire; but a
prophet is only a vessel. You hear his words; but do
you ever stop to wonder where they come from?

TIGLATH: From the gods, of course.

[*He starts impatiently toward the terrace.*]

JONAH [*desperately*]:   Perhaps. Certainly he would like
to think so. May I think that you have followed my
career during the last decade?

TIGLATH: I know your prophecies very well; I could
even recite them to you. The war against Rabbath—
the King of Rabbath had no army—

JONAH: A fact which my wife pointed out to me,
Sire.

TIGLATH [*he is surprised; but he doesn't quite believe it*]:
The series on Egypt—was that your wife's idea, too?
[JEZEBEL *drops her eyes modestly*] [*slowly*] The ora-
tion to the grain merchants?

AZARIAH [*quickly*]:   The great sermon on the divine right of kings—

MIRIAM [*eagerly*]:   The weather prophecies—

AZARIAH: The war with Judah—

JONAH: You see, Your Majesty?

TIGLATH [*wonderingly*]:   Do you mean to tell me that all these years while you were exalting Israel, it was your wife who—who—

JEZEBEL [*simply*]:   Yes, Your Majesty.

JONAH: You recognized the style, Sire, but not the author.

TIGLATH: Well, I'll be . . .

JONAH: She always said: People should be told what is best for them.

TIGLATH: Did she? Did she, indeed?

MIRIAM: You certainly did, Jez. You absolutely did.

AZARIAH: She really did, Your Majesty.

TIGLATH: Well, well! One never knows what's behind a great man. By the Bull! It turns out to be a woman. I wouldn't have believed it.

REBECCA [*seating herself*]:   Is no woman ever born great? Only men?

COLONEL: Silence! Speak when you are spoken to! Besides—we do not sit in the Imperial Presence. Up!

[REBECCA *rises rebelliously*.]

TIGLATH: No one is born great. You have to learn. [*to* JEZEBEL] So *you're* the one I have to thank for that last winds-of-heaven speech?

JEZEBEL [*bold but scared*]:   Yes.

TIGLATH: That was really a corker. It told us all we needed to know—that you people were trusting to dreams again, instead of chariots. Still,—it was a powerful speech. By the Bull! Perhaps we don't need your husband after all.

JEZEBEL [*flustered*]:   But—Your Majesty—

TIGLATH [*for the first time taking a really good look at her*]:   Why not *a woman?* The idea rather appeals to me—

JEZEBEL [*alarmed*]:   I . . . really, Your Majesty—

TIGLATH [*walking around her, studying her*]:   I've got men enough, anyway . . . Hmm—you look a little peaked. You're not poorly, are you?

JONAH: Never had a day's sickness in her life, Your Majesty. Sound as a bell.

TIGLATH [*to the* ASSYRIAN]:   Not a bad figure of a woman . . . Feed her up a little—

JEZEBEL [*uncertainly*]:   Well . . . thank you . . .

TIGLATH: How do you like to travel? By litter? Or horse-back?

JEZEBEL [*with a small show of spirit*]:   I don't know that I care to travel at all.

TIGLATH [*gently*]:   So? [*to the* ASSYRIAN] She has spirit. [*to* JEZEBEL] There is room for a woman of spirit in Nineveh.

JEZEBEL: I'm very comfortable here, thank you.

TIGLATH: There's such a thing as too much spirit. [*look-*

ing around him] However, let's not quarrel. A woman of your possibilities is wasted in a little buffer state like this.

JONAH: A woman is never wasted, Sire.

TIGLATH [*sharply*]:   Never?

JONAH: Not in the right hands, Your Majesty.

TIGLATH [*pleased*]:   Oh. Quite so. Very good; very good. Harubabel—write that down!

JEZEBEL [*as* TIGLATH *goes upstage toward* HARUBABEL]: Jonah! What are you . . . ?

JONAH: His Majesty is right. There's no greatness left in Israel, my dear; there's nothing left for you to work at any more. Her king a fugitive—her prophets dishonored. The world belongs to Nineveh now. From whom all blessings flow.

[*They both bow to* TIGLATH, *as he comes down again.*]

JEZEBEL: I congratulate you. And what will *you* do— when the blessings flow in Nineveh?

JONAH: I shall go back to the desert again, Jezebel—and start all over.

JEZEBEL [*with a side glance at* JUDITH]:   I can imagine with whom. [*she gathers herself together*] [*turning to* TIGLATH] What is Assyria like, Your Majesty—if one *were* to think of . . .

TIGLATH: Assyria . . . It's like thunder and the sound of mountains. A city of porphyry and marble, terra cotta, chalcedony . . . And the bright blue wind of heaven over it. A thousand temples with their fragrance; and the great bazaars. Broad avenues; and endless chariots.

JEZEBEL [*rousing herself a little*]: Are there palaces there? Of gold and bronze?

TIGLATH: You shall have one of ivory and silver.

JEZEBEL: With my own servants?

TIGLATH: Whatever you want.

JEZEBEL: Shall I have a title?

TIGLATH: The noblest in the world.

JEZEBEL: I was a Princess of Israel.

TIGLATH: You shall be more than that.

JONAH: You see, my dear—

JEZEBEL [*looks at him half scornfully. Then, as she sees* REBECCA *gesturing to her*]: I want the right of audience—

TIGLATH: Granted.

[REBECCA *is delighted.*]

JEZEBEL: In perpetuity.

TIGLATH [*impatiently*]: In perpetuity.

JEZEBEL [*glancing at* AZARIAH]: The right of coinage and mintage.

TIGLATH [*startled*]: What?

JONAH: She wants to see herself upon a coin, Your Majesty. It is a small matter; I shouldn't boggle over it.

TIGLATH: I see. Very well. The right of coinage and mintage.

[JEZEBEL *sighs with satisfaction.*]

JEZEBEL: I suppose—there are many ladies at court— in Nineveh?

TIGLATH: Yes.

JEZEBEL: Naturally. One would expect you to have many . . . friends. Do you find—time for them all—?

TIGLATH: I assure you—je fais tout mon possible.

JUDITH [*to* JONAH *in surprise*]:   He speaks Phoenician!

TIGLATH [*to* JUDITH]:   Certainly, Madam. I often visit the coast during the season—for the surf bathing. Incognito, of course.

JEZEBEL [*judiciously*]:   I think it might be better to go in state after this. With the proper escort, and the usual honors.

TIGLATH [*taken aback*]:   You do? Why?

JEZEBEL [*firmly*]:   A king should travel like a king. And his ladies like the king's ladies.

TIGLATH [*uncomfortably*]:   I—er—usually go alone.

JONAH [*with quiet sympathy*]:   You *did,* Sire.

TIGLATH: Hmm! . . . Well—I'm off. Call my chariot, Harry, will you? [*to* JEZEBEL] The councillor and I are off to Rimmon to get Israel straightened out. Get your things packed. You won't need much—get you a new outfit in Nineveh anyway . . . I'll expect you in fourteen hours. Don't keep me waiting.

JEZEBEL [*brightly*]:   I'll try not to. But I have a lot to do. Run along now . . . [*as he turns to go*] and Tiglath!

TIGLATH [*startled*]:   Yes—my dear?

JEZEBEL: You won't do anything stupid at Rimmon—will you?

TIGLATH AND JONAH [*together*]:   No, I won't—

TIGLATH [*somewhat bewildered at his own complaisance*]:
I don't *think* I will . . . [*to* AZARIAH] Come on—let's
go—[*calling*] Chariot! Chariot!

[*He goes out in a hurry.*]

AZARIAH [*in a quick aside to* JEZEBEL]:   When you get to
Nineveh—if you could use any used chariots—

JEZEBEL [*shocked—but amused*]:   Azariah!

AZARIAH: Bless you—

[*He hurries out after* TIGLATH.]

[*Meanwhile* JUDITH *turns hopefully and eagerly to* JONAH
—*but he only shakes his head gently, and she turns sadly
away.*]

JEZEBEL [*cheerfully*]:   Well—who's going to help me
pack? Becky? Miriam?

REBECCA: I think I'll get along home, Jezebel. It's a long
trip—and it's been a confusing day. But if you ever feel
like coming and talking to my organization—or what's
left of it . . . on Woman's Opportunity Today—

[*She goes out twirling her slingshot.*]

MIRIAM: Well—back to the rough and tumble. Take
care of yourself, Jez . . . I know you will.

JEZEBEL: What will *you* do, Mamie?

MIRIAM: Oh—I'll go back to my own little king—poor
soul. He hasn't got much left—except me. Drop me a
line now and then, Jez—from the new world.

JEZEBEL: I will, darling.

MIRIAM: 'Bye, Jonah.

JONAH: Goodbye Miriam.

MIRIAM: 'Bye, Mrs. Hiram. Have fun.

[*She goes out.* JEZEBEL *goes to the terrace to wave her on her way.*]

JUDITH: Goodbye, Lady Miriam . . . [*turning to* JONAH *—sadly*] Well—?

JONAH [*heavily*]:   Well—?

JUDITH: I guess it's time to say goodbye, Johnny.

JONAH: I'll go as far as the gate with you.

JUDITH: No—don't. It's better this way. I'm all right. Come to me when you're ready, darling. I'll wait. We've got a lot of time—[*half laughing and half crying*] We've twenty whole years ahead of us . . . remember? A lot can happen in twenty years, darling— nations can die and blow away. But love just waits.

[*She goes out across the portico, L. as* JEZEBEL *turns in from the terrace R.*]

JEZEBEL: Well, Jonah? What are *you* going to do?

JONAH: Find myself a nice dry cave somewhere—to begin with.

JEZEBEL: I thought you hated caves.

JONAH: I do.

JEZEBEL: Well? After that?

JONAH [*simply*]:   I hope to hear from an old acquaintance, Jezebel. No one you know.

JEZEBEL: Still trying to be friends with someone who doesn't want you! I'd stick to Mrs. Hiram, if I were you. But if you *are* going to live in a cave—be sure to take some warm underwear with you. And you might send me last year's income tax reports; you never understood them anyway. I'll have the Assyrian officials

go over them. And Jonah—for heaven's sake, get your
hair cut—

JONAH [*firmly*]:   Goodbye, Jezebel.

JEZEBEL: I have great plans for Nineveh. You could
have shared them.

JONAH: I know—I could have been a great man. But
the world is a quarrel of birds; and to be great in it is
to be lonely.

JEZEBEL: No wonder God had you swallowed by a
whale!

[*She sweeps indignantly up the stairs. At the same time*
MICAH *comes out, L. and crosses him.*]

JONAH [*taking* MICAH's *staff*]:   Micah!

MICAH: Yes, Jonah?

JONAH: I won't be seeing you again.

MICAH [*dully*]:   They're taking me to Nineveh.

JONAH: Will you let them?

MICAH: Where else have I to go?

JONAH: To your own people.

MICAH: It's too late.

JONAH: It's not too late. They need you, Micah; they
need someone they can trust, to tell them to be of good
heart. To tell them to put away their spears, to beat
their swords into plowshares . . .

MICAH [*incredulously*]:   *Me* tell them that?

JONAH: To sit each man under his own vine and fig tree
again . . .

MICAH: Jonah . . . *How do you know?*

JONAH: How does anyone know . . . [*suddenly realiz-*

111

ing what he is saying] Good Lord! . . . [*he takes off his ring and holds it out to* MICAH] Here's my ruby. Take it to the King; he'll know I sent you.

[*He embraces* MICAH, *and turns in eager wonder to the white feather on the wall. He lifts it from its case, and holds it aloft in triumph.*]

JONAH: Micah—run after Mrs. Hiram. Tell her—that Somebody spoke to me again!

MICAH: And if she says—when will she see you, Jonah?

JONAH [*joyously*]:   Tell her—tell her . . . [*he looks aloft again, and his face falls. It is apparent that Somebody hasn't finished talking to him. When he speaks, it is with more humility. He is still happy; but there is still a ways to go.*] Tell her—week ends and holidays.

MICAH *hurries out; and* JONAH *stands by himself, staring at the feather, a little blessed and a little frightened to feel God's hand upon his shoulder again, as*

THE CURTAIN FALLS

The Sleeping Beauty

CHARACTERS

A WATCHMAN

GEORGE, *a hard-bitten, overworked, assistant director*

EDDIE, *a disappointed screenwriter*

ALBERT, *a young, ignorant, hopeful, brash assistant to an assistant*

EDGAR VARITY, *an ex-director, rather more than middle-aged, somewhat European, definitely Satanic*

THE VOICE OF THE DIRECTOR, *low, commanding, agreeable*

ANNA, *young, reasonably pretty, prim, with a flat voice, middle-class ideals, and no experience*

JOHN ANDERSON, *a middle-aged star*

VANE LAVERNE, *a middle-aged star*

WARDROBE

PROPS

CAMERA MAN

GAFFER

MIXER

MAKE-UP

CONNIE, *Miss LaVerne's stand-in*

HAIR DRESSER

WAITRESS

CAMERA CREW

SOUND CREW

GRIPS

HEAD WAITER

SCRIPT GIRL

FIGURES OF THE NIGHT
[*Bobby Soxers, two flashy babes and their escorts, milkman, photographers, etc.*]

ACT I

The curtain rises on a sound stage on a HOLLYWOOD *studio lot. Portable dressing rooms in back, catwalks overhead, two wooden parallels with unlighted arcs to audience Right, an electric equipment chest, a telephone on a table, a few camp chairs. In the background, a red light, suggesting the door: it blinks on and off. At back, to audience Left, a cyclorama, half-lighted, suggesting a view of the city of* LOS ANGELES. *Off stage, Left, arcs are brilliantly lit, where a scene is being shot out of sight. A* WATCHMAN, *dressed as a studio policeman, sits by himself, Center; he reads a newspaper. Off stage, Left, there is a quiet hum of voices.*

ASSISTANT DIRECTOR [*O.S.*]: All right—quiet. This is a take. Quiet, please, everybody, quiet.
[*The voice stops: It is vacuum-still. A woman from the hair dressing department comes to the door of a dressing room, and stares incuriously off stage at the take. The light stops blinking, and turns red, steadily, with a slight hum.*]
DIRECTOR'S VOICE [*O.S.*]: All right . . . This is a take. Ready? . . . Roll 'em . . .

MIXER'S VOICE [*O.S.*]:   Speed.

[*There is a buzz from the camera.*]

DIRECTOR [*O.S.*]:   Action.

[*There is an intense silence for ten seconds.*]

    Cut . . .

[*The hum of talk starts again.*]

    Print it.

[*The set breaks up. People cross the stage, going slowly toward the right, talking together, or moving props. The star,* JOHN ANDERSON, *in medieval clothes, goes to his dressing room; the feminine co-star,* VENUS LAVERNE, *also in medieval dress, goes to hers. The* HAIRDRESSER *follows her into her room. The* ASSISTANT DIRECTOR *crosses the stage toward the right, talking earnestly to the* SCREEN WRITER. *They are studying a sheet of paper. They talk together, but cannot be heard, above the general hum of conversation. People call out to one another, both on and off stage.*]

AD LIB: Hey—Ed.

    Move that arc—

    Watch it—

    Set 'em up over here—

    Tom . . . where's Tom—?

    Bring that mike over—

    Where's wardrobe?

[*The telephone rings. A man answers it, calls*]

    Hey—Bob—

[*The* GAFFER *comes up, takes it, listens.*]

THE GAFFER: Yeah—Yeah . . . Okay.

[*He puts down the receiver and goes off. The* ASSISTANT DIRECTOR *and* SCRIPTWRITER *stop just before they leave the stage, R.*]

EDDIE (SCRIPTWRITER): You know what *I* like? Count Fleet in the fifth.

ASSISTANT DIRECTOR: Could be. [*He makes a mark on the paper.*] Put ten on him for me.

[*They go out. Meanwhile, during all this,* ANNA *a waitress in the studio commissary, has come slowly in from R., rear. She carries a tray, with a pot of coffee, and a sandwich. She doesn't seem to know her way around very well. She is shy, young, and ill at ease, but at the same time very much interested and excited at finding herself on a set. She is obviously new at the studio. As the stage begins to empty, she approaches the* WATCHMAN, *who hasn't moved. He looks up at her in a bored way.*]

WATCHMAN: Yeah? What you got?

ANNA [*shyly*]: They sent me down with this. [WATCHMAN *peers at the tray.*] For Mr. Anderson.

WATCHMAN [*motioning with his thumb toward the star's dressing room*]: Over there—

[ANNA *nods, and goes over to the dressing room. The door is closed; she doesn't know what to do. She looks questioningly at the* WATCHMAN, *who tells her in pantomime to knock on the door. She nods gratefully, and does so. The door opens, and the star,* JOHN ANDERSON, *looks out; he is still in his full medieval regalia: She stares at him in wonder.*]

ANDERSON: Come in, child.

[*He holds the door open, and ushers her in; the door closes behind her. The* WATCHMAN *watches this with a knowing leer; then, with a sigh, returns to his paper.* VARITY, *the ex-Director, enters from R. Center; he goes up to the* WATCHMAN, *and quietly knocks his hat off.*]

VARITY [*he speaks with a slightly foreign accent*]:   Pop . . . How are you?

WATCHMAN: Eh? . . . Oh . . . it's you, Mr. Varity.

VARITY: Yah . . . it's me. I thought I'd stop by and take a look. How are things going?

WATCHMAN: All right, I guess.

VARITY [*knowingly*]:   They got a good director on it now . . . hey, Pop?

WATCHMAN [*uncomfortably*]:   Well . . . I wouldn't say he was any better than you, Mr. Varity.

VARITY [*smiling*]:   Go on—say it, Pop. I've got another picture anyway. It don't hurt my feelings. [*looking around*] Haven't they broken yet? It's after six—

WATCHMAN: We're shooting till nine tonight.

VARITY [*nodding*]:   So. Are they still calling it The Sleeping Beauty?

WATCHMAN: So far as I know.

VARITY: I never liked it. I'm glad they took me off it.

WATCHMAN: You had a lot of hard luck, Mr. Varity—

VARITY: You still have your charm, Pop. You still have that Irish charm.

WATCHMAN: Sure, Mr. Varity. Sure. Nuts to you.

VARITY: Nuts to you too. Were you ever taken off a picture, Pop?

WATCHMAN: Who, me? I just sit here to keep the girls from getting in each other's hair.

VARITY: Don't ever try to rise in the world then. [*shrugs*] So what am *I* complaining? I've got another picture—with plenty of guts to it. Not like this. Where's Anderson?

WATCHMAN [*motioning to the dressing room*]: He's got someone with him.

VARITY: Anybody I know?

WATCHMAN: Nah, a dame.

VARITY [*astounded*]: Right in the middle of the night like that?

WATCHMAN: It's only just six o'clock. It's his supper.

VARITY [*unbelieving*]: Go on . . .

[*The door of* ANDERSON'S *dressing room opens, and* ANNA *comes out, with her tray. She is quiet, and demure.*]

ANNA: I won't forget, Mr. Anderson.

ANDERSON [*from inside the room*]: That's right, my dear. Hot milk, after this—not cream.

ANNA: I'll remember—

[*She comes downstage with her tray, and goes off, quietly.* VARITY *stares after her.*]

VARITY [*looking after her*]: Who is that?

WATCHMAN [*indifferently*]: I don't know . . . a girl from the commissary—

[VARITY *glances at the dressing room, then starts out after* ANNA. *The door of* MISS LAVERNE'S *dressing room opens, and she comes out, with her* HAIRDRESSER.]

LAVERNE [*to the* WATCHMAN]: How long for supper, Pop?

WATCHMAN [*taking out an old-fashioned watch*]: Forty minutes—

[LAVERNE *looks at her dresser, and shrugs.*]

LAVERNE: Time for an egg. Come on.

[*She leads the way off, R. As she goes across the stage, an* ASSISTANT CAMERAMAN *comes in from the R, and looks up toward the cat-walks.*]

CAMERAMAN: Hey—Bill! Kill the stage lights a minute, will you? I want to run some film—

A VOICE FROM ABOVE: Okay—

[*He goes on toward the L, and off. There is a click, and the stage darkens suddenly; then slowly grows darker. The red door light continues to glow. A baby spot picks up a corner of the stage, R, at first dimly; then a little brighter.* ANNA *is standing in front of a locker; she takes off her apron, hangs it in the locker, takes a cheap jacket from the hook, and puts it over her shoulders. Then she looks at her face in her compact, shrugs, and turns away. She is tired, and dull. Another* WAITRESS *comes on, and starts to open a locker.*]

WAITRESS: Tired, kid? [ANNA *nods*] It's the climate— It's very treacherous. You'd ought to take vitamins.

ANNA: Good night—

WAITRESS: Good night, dear—See you tomorrow—

[ANNA *nods dully, and goes out, into the darkness upstage. The light fades out at R. A lamp post lights up faintly center stage, near the red light;* ANNA *walks slowly and wearily past it, toward L, and is lost in the darkness again. A whistle is heard; it is that of a young man, innocent, joyful and hopeful—but not very tuneful. Figures of the California night drift by: A young couple dreaming, their arms around each other; a woman in a fur coat with a dog on a leash; two men smoking; a middle-aged woman in slacks with her market basket; and a young girl hurrying. A whistle is heard again, and also far-off night sounds, faint auto horns, and a snatch of music. The fog rolls in over the light; the quality of the light changes. It suggests early dawn in the fog. A boy goes by with an armful of newspapers, a milkman with his bottles. The light grows brighter, the street lamp darkens out, and the cyclorama at the left lights up slowly, to its ordinary daytime color, and the stage with it.*]

[*The* ASSISTANT DIRECTOR *and the* SCRIPTWRITER *are sitting around a table, playing gin rummy. The whistle is heard again; and* ALBERT, *the Assistant's assistant, comes from L. He is very young, disorderly, unprepossessing; he has very little in his favor. He carries a large medieval sword.*]

ALBERT: Hey fellers . . . they say they can't use this.

ASSISTANT: Who says they can't?

ALBERT: Anderson. It gets caught in his legs.

ASSISTANT: What's he want—a butter knife? That's what the script calls for—[*to the* WRITER] Don't it,

123

Eddie? A two-handed sword. Correct me if I'm wrong.

EDDIE: Sure. I could have written in a hand grenade, only this is a fairy story.

ALBERT: Look—don't blame me—

ASSISTANT: Nobody's blaming you. Take it easy. Where's props?

ALBERT: They say they got to get an okay to change it—

ASSISTANT: Okay, okay . . . Here, give it to me. I'll take it myself.

[*He gets up, takes the sword, and goes out.* ALBERT *sighs, and sits down in his vacated camp chair.*]

ALBERT: A dog's life.

EDDIE: You think *you* got it tough? Try to be a writer around here.

ALBERT [*earnestly*]: I wouldn't ever want to try that. That sort of thing is beyond me. I don't see how you guys ever think up the . . .

EDDIE [*laying out a hand of Canfield*]: Sure—sure. I know. And soforth and soforth . . . Say—who's the babe keeps bringing Anderson his lunch every day?

ALBERT: Girl named Anna. From the commissary. Why?

EDDIE [*winks*]: Oh boy!

ALBERT [*it hadn't occurred to him*]: You think so?

EDDIE: I think what?

ALBERT: *You* know—

EDDIE [*scornfully*]: With Anderson? Nah! [*quoting*] "Euclid alone has looked on Beauty bare" [*he plays solitaire*] She's a dish, though.

ALBERT: I don't go for the type much myself.

EDDIE [*absently*]:   What type, kid?

ALBERT: Oh—you know . . . school-girl stuff. I like 'em hot.

EDDIE [*smiling*]:   "I cried for madder music and stronger wine . . . I have been faithful to thee, Cynara, in my fashion." Me, I figure a woman's a woman, she's either asleep or awake, and when she's awake, brother watch out!

ALBERT [*pointing to the cards*]:   You got a red five on a black six.

EDDIE [*playing it*]:   Yeah—thanks. Leave me make my own mistakes.

[*He plays quietly.* ALBERT *watches him.*]

[*The* ASSISTANT DIRECTOR *comes in, L.*]

ASSISTANT: Okay—you guys going to lunch?

EDDIE: So early?

ASSISTANT: We got a big lighting job will take almost an hour, so he says we should eat now—

EDDIE: I just had breakfast. Who does he think he is— God?

ASSISTANT: You said it, boy. A director is God.

ALBERT: What's an assistant director's assistant?

ASSISTANT: You know the front end of a horse?

ALBERT: Yeah . . . ?

ASSISTANT: Well . . . Aah, skip it. Come on, kid.

ALBERT [*rising*]:   Okay . . .

EDDIE [*rising, throwing down his cards*]:   One of these days I'm going to do this thing without cheating.

[*They go out. A cold light plays on the outside of* ANDER-

son's *dressing room. The door opens, and* VARITY *stands
negligently in the doorway, smoking a cigarette. He looks
R, sees someone coming, and his face lights up with
interest.* ANNA *comes in from R, with a tray. She is a
little taken aback to find* VARITY *blocking the doorway.*]

ANNA: I got Mr. Anderson's lunch.

VARITY: He isn't here.

ANNA [*turning away*]: Oh . . .

VARITY: Wait a minute. What have you got? [*looking
at the tray*] Noodle soup—date salad. Bring it in. I'll
eat it.

ANNA [*troubled*]: I don't know if I can do that—

VARITY: It's all right. I'll sign for it—

[*He steps aside to let her in. She enters submissively
with her tray; he closes the door after her.*]

[*A crew of grips comes across stage in front of the
door, pushing a couple of light towers before them. They
go to stage right. A* SOUND MAN *brings his mike over; the
stage lights up, R, as the arcs are plugged in.* PROP MEN
*start arranging the scene; they bring on a very fancy
looking bed. It is large and medieval—the bed of a princess, all in damask and silk. The* WATCHMAN *strolls over
to watch.*]

DIRECTOR'S VOICE [*O.S.*]: Where's Connie? Where's La-
Verne's stand-in? . . . Oh, there you are. All right,
darling . . . on the bed.

[*A girl looking vaguely like* MISS LAVERNE *comes out
of wings, R, and goes to the bed. She lies down on it.*]

GAFFER'S VOICE [*O.S.*]: Hit your arcs.

[*Lights go on brightly from above.*]

DIRECTOR [*O.S.*]:   I want the camera to come in slowly.
[*The* CAMERAMAN *comes out with a light meter, holds it
to the girl's face. A* CAMERA ASSISTANT *comes out with a
tape measure, and measures the distance between the
girl and the off-stage camera. The* SOUND MAN *tests the
movement of his mike. A* PROP MAN *comes out with more
pillows. The* CAMERAMAN *calls to the men on the cat-
walk overhead and out of sight.*]

CAMERAMAN: Not so hot on the Left . . . We want a
silk over there. [*A* GRIP *sets up a silk screen in front
of one of the mounted arcs. The* CAMERAMAN *judges
and ponders, cocking his head from side to side, walking from one part of the set to another. He waves signals to the men overhead, to lower or brighten their
arcs. The girl on the bed stirs restlessly, scratches herself and yawns.*] [*to the girl*] Just a little while, dear
. . . [*calling to the* ASSISTANT CAMERA *O.S.*] That
shadow all right?

ASSISTANT CAMERA [*O.S.*]:   Not quite . . . Try a net.

GAFFER [*calling up*]:   Put a net on five . . . that's it . . .
Okay . . . All right—cut your arcs—

[*The bright lights go out suddenly as the arcs are cut.
The entire stage darkens somewhat; the girl gets off the
bed, and the crew wanders off the stage, R. At the same
time, light comes on inside the dressing room; we see
into it, through a transparent screen.* VARITY *is sitting on
the couch, and* ANNA *sits opposite him on the chair.*
VARITY *is finishing his lunch.*]

VARITY: You see . . . after all—I know a good deal about you. That's the business of a director—to know about people. For instance . . . I know your name is Anna Cawley, and that you live alone—at 1247 Jasmine Street. Right?

ANNA [*uncomfortably*]: I don't know why you want to know about me—

VARITY: I just told you. I've been going about the earth and walking up and down in it . . . You interest me. I ask myself—are you alive?

ANNA: All directors are crazy, I guess—

VARITY: All *ex*-directors . . . fallen angels, ex-seraphim, past-captains-of-the-Hosts . . . What do you talk about with Mr. Anderson, when you bring him his lunch?

ANNA [*defensively*]: I don't talk about anything—

VARITY: Do you mean that you just sit there and stare at him? How does he take it?

ANNA: Oh—he says things sometimes—

VARITY: Like what?

ANNA: Like . . . like what did I use to do back home in Minnesota—

VARITY: What *did* you do in Minnesota, Miss Cawley?

ANNA: I was a waitress.

VARITY: At least you're consistent. You were a waitress in Minnesota; so now you are a waitress in Hollywood. Don't you ever want to be anything else?

ANNA: What's it to you?

128

VARITY: Nothing . . . Don't you ever want to be famous? And have your picture in the papers?

ANNA [*simply*]: Why?

VARITY: Why—to send back home to Minnesota, I suppose.

ANNA: I wouldn't know how you did that.

VARITY: There are ways.

ANNA [*dully*]: Like what?

VARITY: It is a question of being seen with the right people—

ANNA [*dispiritedly*]: Me?

VARITY [*warming up to it*]: In the right places. You are at Ciro's, dining and dancing. Flash bulbs are going off, pop pop—the gossips are busy—you are looking up into his face—everybody is wondering who you are—

ANNA [*dully*]: You like to make jokes, don't you?

VARITY [*taken aback*]: Jokes? Maybe. But the whole world is a joke, Miss Cawley. Would you like to know what is *really* a joke? That Edgar Varity, who won the International Award in Vienna two years in succession . . . two years, mind you! . . . should be taken off a picture like The Sleeping Beauty which in any case is a turkey. No—that is something that is *really* a joke, Miss Cawley . . . much funnier than that some hopeful little waitress from Minnesota gets her face in the papers! Believe me. No.

ANNA: You don't have to insult me.

VARITY [*taken aback*]: Insult you? So I have insulted you? [*he strikes his forehead*] Yoh! I have insulted her!

ANNA [*rising*]: Are you finished with the tray?

[*She holds out her hand for it.* VARITY *gives it to her; he is in some confusion of mind.*]

VARITY: Yes, I'm finished—but look here—I am interested. You say I have insulted you. How?

ANNA [*takes the tray, and starts out. Quietly*]: You don't have to make fun of me, either. [*She comes down the steps of the dressing room, the transparent curtain becomes opaque again, showing the outside of the room; she starts across the stage, carrying the tray. meanwhile, during the end of the last scene, several grips have come on, R, and set up a hedge around the bed, suggesting the overgrown brambles and bushes of The Sleeping Beauty's castle.* ANNA *blunders into this; and finds her way blocked. Puzzled, she turns from one side to another, only to find more brambles, set out by the grips.*] [*in a mild panic*] How do I get out of here?

A GRIP: You hadn't ought to be in here, lady—

[ANNA *looks helplessly at her tray. She turns blindly, and starts toward the wings, only to be blocked by an arc light stand which is pushed in her way. As she backs away from it, she half falls against a sound-mike, and then trips over a wire cable, and sits down hard, with a clatter of dishes.*]

ANNA: Oh—!

[ALBERT *comes from the shadows, L, and looks at her in surprise.*]

ALBERT: What you doing? Did you trip over something?

ANNA [*angrily scrambling to her feet*]: What do you think I did? [*she tries to gather her dishes together, but she has to stop to rub her knee*] Ow!

ALBERT: Did you hurt yourself?

ANNA [*looks at him scornfully*]: That forest wasn't here before—

ALBERT [*picking up a cup*]: Here's a cup—

ANNA [*hobbling a little toward him*]: Thanks.

ALBERT: Gee, you hurt yourself, didn't you. Go on—sit down a minute, and take it easy . . . Here—

[*He leads her to the bed, and after a moment's hesitation, she sinks down on it. She starts to rub her knee again;* ALBERT *gazes at it with interest.*]

ANNA: I must have pulled something—

ALBERT: Yeah—you want to be careful how you fall around here. You could break a leg or something.

ANNA: That's fine—

ALBERT: I broke an arm once. Skating. Came down wham; bust it in three places. I had bits of bone sticking out right through the skin.

ANNA [*wincing*]: Through the skin?

ALBERT [*with relish*]: Right through the skin. I was a pretty good skater, too; but I broke my arm. It's amazing how delicate people are. That's why I say you want to be careful how you fall.

ANNA: You've got to be careful about more than that around here.

ALBERT [*nodding wisely*]: Somebody make a pass at you?

ANNA: What gave you that idea?

ALBERT [*airily*]: Oh—nothing . . . but you know—you've been sort of coming around.

ANNA: Just doing my job. And minding my business.

ALBERT: Meaning—leave me do likewise?

ANNA: Meaning that.

ALBERT: I get it. Only you can't keep people from thinking things—

ANNA: People are always thinking things. Thinking and asking . . . They never believe you, either. They want to know what you're after all the time; they want to know what you want. Only maybe you don't know what you want. Then they don't believe you. Like I told this man, this director, Mr. Varity I think is his name. So he suggested I go out and get my picture taken dancing at Ciro's!

ALBERT: At Ciro's? Holy Cow!

ANNA: That's what I said. Why, I said, that's an insult. No insult intended, he said. Imagine that!

ALBERT: I don't get it. Who was insulting who?

ANNA: He was insulting me, is who. Me—at Ciro's!

ALBERT [*uncertainly*]: Well . . . *I* don't know . . .

ANNA: Some girls are serious, that's all; they don't want to be made a joke out of, about certain things.

ALBERT: Suppose he was serious?

ANNA: Don't be silly.

ALBERT: No—really; suppose a fellow was serious, and asked you to go out dancing with him . . . I don't mean a place like Ciro's—but—

ANNA [*stonily*]: I don't go out with people I don't know—

ALBERT [*boldly*]: You know me, don't you?

ANNA [*rising*]: I don't know you. And anyway—even if I did know you—

ALBERT [*hopeful*]: Yes?—

ANNA: I'd have to think about it.

[*She leaves.*]

ALBERT [*calling after her*]: Well—think about it—will you?

[*He follows her out.*]

[*As she goes, the* ASSISTANT DIRECTOR *and* PROP MAN *comes in from L.* PROP MAN *carries a sack.*]

PROP: All I know is, the chief wants to see the ornaments. He says they got to be medieval. You know—nothing like from a modern jeweler.

ASSISTANT: Okay, okay, what you got?

PROP: Here. [*He stops, and opens his sack, and begins taking out costume jewelry. He hands one or two pieces to the* ASSISTANT, *who glances at them carelessly.*] Here's a crown—I figure maybe she ought to have a crown—?

ASSISTANT: She's asleep, isn't she? What did she do—go to sleep with her crown on?

PROP: You think she took it off? I got a wife, I gave her

a fur coat last Christmas, by God if she don't go to bed that night with her coat on!

ASSISTANT: So what? You put the girl to bed in a fur coat, and the Breen office will cut it right out of the picture, because it's liable to suggest God knows what to some school girl in Alabama.

PROP: This is a crown, not a fur coat—

ASSISTANT: Yeah—Well, we got enough headaches without going to bed with no crown on. [PROP *sighs and puts the crown slowly back in the bag*] [*carelessly*] Leave the junk—I'll show it to the chief.

[PROP *puts the jewelry down on the bed, as* VARITY *comes out of* ANDERSON's *dressing room, and approaches them.*]

VARITY: Gentlemen . . . How are you, George?—

ASSISTANT [*whose name is* GEORGE] [*surprised*]:   Hi ya, Mr. Varity. Haven't seen you for a long time—

VARITY: When Lucifer was cast down from the heavens, he did not turn up again until after the Creation. Then he turned up in the Garden of Eden. [*looking at the set*] I am right at home here.

GEORGE: This is no Garden of Eden.—

VARITY: On the contrary, George—every day looks like paradise—if you get up early enough. We have forgotten the morning look of the world.

PROP: Excuse me—[*to* GEORGE] I'll be seeing you.

[*He goes off R.*]

GEORGE: Yeah—see you . . . [*to* VARITY] I'm on the set every day at 7:30. That's morning enough for me.

VARITY: It isn't good enough. You come here full of coffee, with your eyes half open, already irritable and worried. But at five o'clock, when the sun is just rising, you are blameless and innocent . . . snoring like a buzz saw.

GEORGE: Not last night, brother! I was playing poker with the boys.

VARITY: And what more innocent than that? Man without woman is as blameless as a male mosquito.

GEORGE: And women without men?

VARITY: There never *was* a woman without a man. Eve was made from Adam's rib; so already there was a man in the world. [*looking at the bed*] What have you there? The jewels of the kingdom?

GEORGE: We got to dress LaVerne up to look like a princess. You can imagine.

VARITY [*idly handling the jewels*]: I could never see why they chose LaVerne to be the Sleeping Beauty. There are so many sleeping beauties in the world . . . and LaVerne has been awake for a long time. I would have taken an unknown . . . a girl maybe who was a waitress in Minnesota . . . and still asleep—

GEORGE: Not box office—

VARITY: I know—I know. But it would be interesting! And real. And then—when she wakes up—ha! That also would be interesting.

GEORGE: They're all alike—

VARITY: But like what? That is the thing. Do they eat their husbands, like the spider? Or are they like the bee, for whom one embrace is enough for a lifetime? Or are they like the virus, about which we know nothing? I am curious about such things. That is why I do not like to make fairy stories.

GEORGE: I hear you got a new picture—

VARITY: Yes. It is real. It has guts. We open in a storm drain; we hear shots—a-a-a-a-a . . . figures escape through the shadows. Powerful, huh?

GEORGE [*wearily*]:   Sure. And the detective and the girl get together in the fade-out.

VARITY: It is the district attorney. But who cares? All through the ten reels we have been shooting a-a-a-a-a, sirens wa-a-a-a-a, people running, cars going around corners, women screaming, fists going bing-bang . . . It is real, hah? It is powerful. [*suddenly with great bitterness*] Like limburger cheese!

GEORGE: Aaah—they go for that sort of junk—

VARITY [*regaining his airy good humor*]:   Well—It's a job . . . Here's Beauty's prince himself—Hello John—

[*As* ANDERSON *comes on from R, eating a hot dog.*]

ANDERSON: Hello, Edgar—What are *you* doing over here? I thought they'd fixed you up at RKO—

VARITY: We haven't started shooting yet. They can't decide who owns the studio.

ANDERSON: Well—we have no such trouble around here. This studio is owned by an elderly gentleman in New York who has never written, directed, or produced a picture in his life. He lives three thousand miles away; and what he says, goes.

VARITY: Naturally; at such distance, he has divinity. More than divinity . . . an awful and unapproachable majesty. He is the God beyond God—the unspeakable word, above and beyond Jehovah. Why should he direct? You are like a sparrow, that asks God also to lay an egg. The lesser Gods direct—Jehovah, and—Lucifer.

GEORGE [*to* ANDERSON]:   He hasn't changed any—

ANDERSON: Thank heavens for that . . . there are enough changes in this business. [*looking at the set*] Is this where I come in—through this stuff?

GEORGE: Yeah—

ANDERSON: What is it—poison ivy? [*takes hold of a bramble and pricks his hand*] By God, it's the real stuff! What did they do—bring it in from outside?

VARITY: That is for realism, John. So they will say in Kansas City, look—real brambles.

ANDERSON: They'll scratch the hide off me—

VARITY: It is all for art; we give what we have—which reminds me. I ate your lunch today.

ANDERSON [*looking at the remains of the frankfurter*]: There's my lunch. As far as I know, I ate it myself, old boy. [*throwing the remains to* GEORGE] Throw it away for me, will you George?

GEORGE: Yes, Mr. Anderson—

[*He goes out with the remains of the hot dog.*]

VARITY: That is just your alternate lunch. Your real lunch came to your dressing room as usual, on a tray. I ate it.

ANDERSON [*blankly*]:   Oh . . . you did, eh?

VARITY: You're a sly dog, John—

ANDERSON [*surprised*]:   Why do you say that?

VARITY: The young lady?

ANDERSON: Don't be an ass, old boy.

VARITY [*in unbelief*]:   You mean you are not up to something?

ANDERSON: Are you crazy?

VARITY: You do not fool me, with this display of innocence. I know you too well.

ANDERSON: For heaven's sake—She's a child! A baby! Besides—

VARITY: Besides—what?

ANDERSON [*he picks up the jewels on the bed, and plays with them idly*]:   You're a great troublemaker, old boy.

VARITY: C'est mon metier.

ANDERSON: What are you trying to do? Cook up something between me—and a kid from the commissary? You'd have me out of here on my ear—you know that?

VARITY: On the contrary—it is a romance dear to the American heart. What is the great story in this country? Cinderella.

ANDERSON [*glumly*]:   It ends with marriage, old boy.

VARITY: Let us not be naive. Marriage is a very strong temptation; but its strength is in the past. Today there are many more ways of getting on in the world. [*he takes a bracelet from* ANDERSON's *hand, tosses it in the air, and throws it back on the bed*] Who cares today

138

ALBERT: Yeah, it's responsibility, all right. Have another coke—

[*He fishes one up for her from the floor of the car, and opens it.*]

ANNA: Thank you.

ALBERT: It's nothing . . . I hope you enjoy it. You know what an assistant director is? He's like the horse's head. I'm *his* assistant . . . It's the assistants get things done out here. The big shots just give orders —but who carries them out? That's what *I* want to know.

ANNA: I guess you're right . . . Gee, it really is beautiful up here. Like you were dreaming, or something.

ALBERT: I always wanted to meet a girl like you—you know, one that had appreciation—

ANNA: I always think you can tell about people when you meet them—whether they have nice feelings or not . . . I've always tried to keep my thoughts nice, because you never can tell when you're going to meet —you know—somebody—

ALBERT [*a trifle husky*]: Did you ever meet—somebody?

ANNA [*slowly*]: I wouldn't want to answer that yet, Albert.

ALBERT: I guess you've had plenty of opportunities.

ANNA: I've lived alone a lot . . . You know, when a girl lives alone there's opportunity for a lot of things. That's not a very refined thing for me to say, is it? When I don't know you very well. But I don't know—

141

I sort of feel I can trust you, Albert. Like you say, you have appreciation.

ALBERT: A man is alone too, you know—

ANNA: It's easier for a man. He doesn't have to wait for things to happen.

ALBERT: Yeah—but suppose he has ideals? You can be a chaser—but what's the percentage?

ANNA: I certainly believe in ideals—You never have to be ashamed if you've got ideals—

ALBERT [*bitterly*]: Most girls don't think that.

ANNA: You just haven't met the right girls, Albert. Probably on account of the profession you're in, I guess. You take a star like Miss LaVerne . . . why she's had three husbands already . . . what sort of ideals is that?

ALBERT [*with relish*]: And boy-friends too, I can tell you—

ANNA [*more firmly*]: The thing I like about you, Albert, is you've got nice feelings . . . I mean, you wouldn't take advantage . . . You know what I mean? You take most people in your profession, they don't have any nice feelings about a girl. They're always after what they can get . . . you know, wanting to hold her hand, and kiss her, and everything . . . [*with a light and very self-conscious laugh*] My goodness, it's all your life is worth—

ALBERT: I guess it is . . .

ANNA: What I mean, you take most fellows, up here all alone like this, why they'd be all over you . . .

ALBERT [*more unhappily*]: Yeah . . .

ANNA: Of course—I suppose they figure what's a kiss now and then? You know . . . if it's done in a nice way—

ALBERT [*miserably*]: Yeah—I guess that's how they figure—

ANNA [*running down*]: Yes—that's the way they figure it.

[*They sit in an uncomfortable silence for a moment.*]

ALBERT [*swallowing, humbly*]: I don't suppose . . . you'd let *me* kiss you—?

ANNA [*coming to life again*]: Why, Albert!

ALBERT [*hoarsely*]: Would you?

ANNA [*slowly and solemnly*]: I'd rather not, Albert. I think things like that should be sincere—don't you?

ALBERT [*unhappily*]: Yeah. Sure.

ANNA: After all, we've only just met—

ALBERT: But I'm sincere, Anna—honest I am!

ANNA: Besides—you wouldn't respect me afterwards—

ALBERT: Yes I would—

[*He leans toward her eagerly.*]

ANNA [*gently pushing him away*]: I haven't made my mind up about you yet, Albert—

ALBERT: I made my mind up about you—

ANNA: How could you, so soon?

ALBERT: Well—I did—

ANNA: How do you know you're sure?

ALBERT: I know it, all right.

ANNA: Aren't you afraid it would spoil something, Albert?

ALBERT [*aggrieved*]:   What could it spoil—for goodness sake?

ANNA: I don't know . . . but—

ALBERT: You said you liked me a little—

ANNA: I do.

ALBERT: Well, then—?

ANNA [*yielding primly*]:   Well . . . just a little one, Albert—

[*In the semi-darkness, they come together. Their part of the stage darkens, but the cyclorama continues to twinkle its lights against the dark blue night-sky. Toward the center of the stage a small set lights up; it is the entrance to a nightclub on the Strip. Music sounds from inside. Five or six* AUTOGRAPH SEEKERS *and* BOBBY-SOXERS *wait hopefully by the entrance. Suddenly the door is flung open, and two "flashy babes" come out, clawing at each other's hair, their escorts come out after them, to try and separate them; there is a certain amount of outcry and confusion; it is a typical cafe brawl. The* DOORMAN *and* MANAGER *also come out, the young ladies, much rumpled, are separated, and each is led off in an opposite direction by her escort. As the* BOBBY-SOXERS, *etc., gaze after the retreating couples, the door opens again, and* VARITY *and* VENUS LAVERNE *come out;* LAVERNE *is, simply, a movie star. She is worth three million a year (gross) to her studio; and is proud to say that she has never known (or met) a writer.* VARITY *is laughing, but* LAVERNE'S* *face betrays nothing, one way or another. It is polite, wide-eyed, and blank. She wears a fur stole.*]

VARITY: Were you entertained, my dear? So much hate and fury—

LAVERNE: Disgusting.

VARITY: That is the tiger, always inside the kitten. It is a good thing not to forget.

LAVERNE: You hadn't ought to have egged them on at each other.

VARITY [*shrugs*]: I like to see the real spite in people . . . Shall we go home?

[*The* AUTOGRAPH-HUNTERS *press forward, holding out their autograph books.*]

BOBBY-SOXERS: Can we have your autograph, Miss La-Verne? . . . your autograph, Miss LaVerne—

[*Smiling a wooden, professional smile, but with a sense of satisfaction,* LAVERNE *signs the books, as the scene darkens out. The stage lights up further to the right, to show a corner of* ANDERSON's *living room.* ANDERSON *sits reading, in a flowered bathrobe.* LAVERNE *comes in, still in her evening gown; she takes off her fur stole and throws it down.*]

LAVERNE: What a boring evening—

ANDERSON [*not looking up from his book*]: Where did you go?

LAVERNE: Cucaracha. The usual fight—and Edgar being very clever all the time . . . [*she sits down wearily*] Why can't we go to Mexico for a while?

ANDERSON [*mechanically*]: Me—hi—co—

LAVERNE: Oh God—don't *you* be clever, too—

ANDERSON [*putting down his book*]: What's the difference? It's just a place.

LAVERNE: Well—what else is there? I'm sick of the same old things—

ANDERSON: Why don't you retire? Give it all up—

LAVERNE: Are you crazy?

ANDERSON [*shrugging*]: What do you expect, then? The same things over again. You've done everything in the world—

LAVERNE [*furiously*]: That's right. Insult me.

ANDERSON: I'm tired of insulting you.

LAVERNE: Why don't you say what you mean?

ANDERSON: All right . . . What do I mean?

LAVERNE: Say it. Say you're tired of me—

ANDERSON [*wearily*]: We're too much alike, that's all. We've had everything; both of us. There are no surprises left for us—in each other.

LAVERNE [*dully*]: We could get married—

ANDERSON: Why?

LAVERNE: I don't know—

ANDERSON: That wouldn't solve anything. It never has.

LAVERNE: You used to say nice things to me, Johnny. You used to say I was the most exciting person you knew—

ANDERSON: You were, once. You would be again—to somebody who didn't know you. So would *I* be . . . to a stranger—

146

LAVERNE: Oh. So there's somebody—already—

ANDERSON: Do I have to remind you that we are *not* married?

LAVERNE: Thank God!

ANDERSON: Ditto.

LAVERNE: I wouldn't marry you if . . .

ANDERSON: I know . . . if I were the last man on earth. As a matter of fact, if I *were* the last man on earth, think how excited you'd be at finding me!

LAVERNE: Oh Johnny—don't let's quarrel. We loved each other! Haven't we got anything left?

ANDERSON: Hunger—for other things.

LAVERNE: You're hateful—

ANDERSON: How many autographs did you sign tonight?

LAVERNE: A dozen—I don't know—twenty—

ANDERSON: I went to Mocambo. I signed fifteen.

LAVERNE: Well—?

ANDERSON: Don't you see? Neither one of us brings home any bacon for the other.

LAVERNE [*hotly*]: What do you mean, bacon?

ANDERSON: We have no pride in each other. We're only proud of ourselves. If you sign more autographs than I do, I hate you.

LAVERNE [*hotly*]: Can I help it if they ask me?

ANDERSON: No—you can't help it. We both want to be told we're great—that we're the apple of everybody's eye. There's only room for one apple in an eye, my dear—

LAVERNE: There's two eyes, aren't there?

ANDERSON: On either side of the face. Separated. By the nose.

LAVERNE [*quietly*]:   I see. [*she rises*] What are you doing? Calling quits?

ANDERSON: Be honest. Wouldn't you be relieved?

LAVERNE: If there's going to be any calling around here, I'll do it. [*she starts for the door*] What's more, I'll know what to call you, too.

ANDERSON: Be sensible—

LAVERNE: Who is she, John?

ANDERSON: I tell you—there isn't anyone.

LAVERNE: Uh—huh. Well—I'll find out. Somebody will tell me—That'll be fine. I'll enjoy that.

ANDERSON [*wearily*]:   Oh—skip it, Vane—

LAVERNE: And when I do—I'll give her something to be proud of.

[*She goes out.* ANDERSON *sighs. He goes to a side table and pours himself a drink. As he holds it up in front of him, the scene darkens out, and the cyclorama at L begins to change color. The lights (many of which have gone out during the above scene) now go out altogether, and the sky begins to take on the first faint colors of early morning. As the colors deepen, and as the entire stage begins to be seen in a grey, pearly, early-morning light, a milkman, carrying his milk bottles, crosses from L to R. As he nears the wings,* GEORGE, *the Assistant Director, comes on from R, and crosses him.* GEORGE *is sleepy, and tousled. He yawns, and stumbles wearily across the*

148

stage, going off L. The cyclorama is now full morning.
He is followed by ALBERT, *who comes in whistling, then*
PROPS *and* EDDIE; PROPS *carries an armful of crowns and*
weapons, EDDIE *is drinking a cup of coffee as he walks.*
GRIPS, WARDROBE, HAIRDRESSER, CAMERAMAN, *the* GAFFER,
SOUND MEN, *the* STAND-IN *for* LAVERNE *all cross the stage*
toward L; they greet each other with occasional grunts
and short remarks—]

AD LIB: Hi ya—

Good morning, Tom—

Hi ya, boy—

Ah—here's another day—

Back to the factory—

What a night—I didn't sleep a wink—

Say—I think we had an earthquake last night. The
bed was rocking—

So this is a cute tomato—

So I said to her, Ma, I said, lay off, will ya?

It's cruel the way they're driving us—etc.

[*The telephone rings. A man answers it.*]

MAN: Yeah? . . . [*calling*] Hey, Bob!

[*The* GAFFER *comes over, takes up the phone, listens.*]

GAFFER: Yeah . . . yeah . . . okay—

[*He puts down the receiver—goes off, L. The* WATCHMAN
comes in, sits down, and starts to read the morning
paper.]

GAFFER [*O.S.*]:   Hit your arcs—

[*The arcs go on, all aimed at a point off-stage, L. The*

*cyclorama is more or less blanked out by them. People
call out, O.S., L.—]*

AD LIB: Hey—Jim—

Move that arc—

Watch it—

Set 'em up over here—

Tom—where's Tom—?

Hey, Eddie—

Move that mike—

ASSISTANT [*O.S.*]:   Quiet! Quiet please.

DIRECTOR'S VOICE [*O.S.*]:   Where's Miss LaVerne? . . .

VOICES [*in the distance*]:   LaVerne . . . On the set—

DIRECTOR [*O.S.*]:   All right, everybody . . . Now we're
going right into the same scene we did last night. I
want a lot more life in it. No rehearsal. This is *not* a
rehearsal. This is a take. Miss LaVerne? Oh—there you
are, darling. Got your lines?

LAVERNE [*O.S.*]:   I think so.

DIRECTOR [*O.S.*]:   Give her the lines—

SCRIPT GIRL [*O.S.*] [*reading*]:   What else is there? I am
tired of the same old things.

DIRECTOR [*O.S.*]:   Got it? Okay . . . Ready? Everybody?

ASSISTANT: Quiet—quiet please. This is a take. Everybody quiet.

DIRECTOR [*O.S.*]:   Roll 'em—

MIXER'S VOICE [*O.S.*]:   Speed.

[*The camera buzzes.*]

DIRECTOR [*O.S.*]:   Action!

[*There is a moment of silence. Then* LaVerne's *voice*—]

LAVERNE [*O.S.*]:   What else is there? I'm tired of the same old things!

DIRECTOR [*O.S.*]:   Cut. Print it.

[THE CURTAIN FALLS QUICKLY.]

ACT II

[*The curtain rises on a black stage. A spot picks out* ANNA, *at R; she is in front of her locker, taking off her jacket, and putting on her apron. As she does so, the other* WAITRESS *comes in to do the same; the two girls greet each other.*]

WAITRESS: 'Morning, dearie—

ANNA: 'Morning—

WAITRESS: Well—another day. You look a little peaked to me. You sleep all right?

ANNA [*coolly*]: Just fine—

WAITRESS: I wish I could. I don't hardly sleep at all. My feet hurt so, from walking on them.

[*She ties her apron on, and goes out.* ANNA *stops to powder her nose, and then follows her. The light goes out in that part of the stage, and a moment later, the full stage lights up; it is as before, except that the cyclorama is obscured by a set. The camera is off, L. Stage lights are on. The* GRIPS *are busy arranging the set, which is a ballroom in a castle—a fairytale ballroom, such as might (not too awkwardly) find itself transformed into*] *a modern night club, at the drop of a curtain. The set reaches to about the center of the stage, and suggests that a large part of it—the main part, in fact—extends out behind the wings, L. There are marble columns, an arched doorway, etc. Arcs stand about; downstage, center, two camp chairs; in the background, as before, are the two dressing rooms. The doors of both are visible. GEORGE, the Assistant Director, is supervising the set arrangements.]*

A GRIP [*bringing in two small upholstered chairs from L*]: You want these here?

[*He starts to set them down toward C.*]

GEORGE: No, no—the corner— [*the grip puts them in the corner*] Now bring that table in—

[*The grip goes out L, and comes in again with a small ornate table. GEORGE fussily arranges the chairs.*]

GRIP: You hadn't ought to do that. That's union work—

GEORGE: Okay—you didn't see me. Here—stick the table down here. The chairs behind it—

GRIP [*holding the table*]: What you want a table in a ballroom?

GEORGE [*his mind on other things*]: It's in the script—ask Eddie—

GRIP [*calling*]: Hey, Eddie—You want a table in the ballroom?

[*Eddie comes on from L.*]

EDDIE: Why not?

GRIP: Oh. [*he shrugs*] Okay.

[*He puts down the table and goes off.*]

EDDIE [*looking after him—to* GEORGE]:   So now the *grips* are trying to write my script for me!

GEORGE: We got too many geniuses out here.

EDDIE: Sure. You start here as a genius, or not at all. So if you're lucky you find maybe you've got a little talent, and you go back East to Cape Cod, and write a book.

GEORGE [*re-arranging the table and chairs*]:   What does a guy get for writing a book, Eddie?

EDDIE: Hemorrhoids.

[*He turns back, L.*]

GEORGE [*calling*]:   Hey—gaffer. Light her up, will you?

GAFFER [*O.S.*]:   Hit your arcs—[*the arcs go on*]

GEORGE [*calling back*]:   Connie—sit down here a minute, will you, dear? [*the stand-in comes out, sits down in one of the chairs. She stares dispiritedly into space.* GEORGE *looks at her, his head to one side. The* CAMERAMAN *comes out and joins him.*] [*calling back*] How's that, Chief?

DIRECTOR [*O.S.*]:   Not bad . . . Try her a little to the right—[GEORGE *moves* CONNIE *more to the right. The* CAMERAMAN *makes signals to the* ELECTRICIANS *overhead.*] That's better . . . Wait till I get a line on it— [*Meanwhile,* ALBERT *and* ANNA *have come on, R.* ANNA *is without her apron; she is self-conscious, and tidying her hair with small, prim, ladylike touches. She glances surreptitiously at* ANDERSON's *dressing room.*]

ALBERT: Come on—don't be afraid.

ANNA: Honest, I haven't any business here, Albert—

ALBERT: Nobody's going to bite you, baby!

ANNA: They might think I was intruding. [*standing still and looking at the stand-in—in a whisper*] Albert —that isn't Miss LaVerne—?

ALBERT: Heck, no! That's her stand-in. Connie, her name is.

ANNA: Oh. I thought she sort of didn't look like La-Verne—

ALBERT: This is a ballroom, where they're going to shoot the big ballroom scene. [*pointing off to L*] See that staircase? Looks like marble, don't it? That's the same staircase was in "The White Cliffs".

ANNA: My. It's beautiful.

ALBERT [*nods happily*]:   See that chandelier? It's real crystal. Gorgeous, hey?

ANNA: It's beautiful.

ALBERT: Going to be a big production. Two hundred extras.

GEORGE [*looking up and seeing* ALBERT]:   Hey—Albert— come over here, will you?

ALBERT [*self-consciously to* ANNA]:   Pardon me—[*he walks over to* GEORGE *and the* CAMERAMAN. *Briskly*—] Yes, sir?

GEORGE [*glancing at him in surprise*]:   Yes, sir? [*he looks at* ANNA, *who turns self-consciously away, then at* ALBERT; *he understands that* ALBERT *is on parade*] Oh. [*then briskly*] Come on, get to work. Tell Eddie we got to talk to him.

[ALBERT *looks anxiously at* ANNA, *whose back, however, is turned.*]

ALBERT: Okay, Chief.

[*He goes off L.* GEORGE *and the* CAMERAMAN *start more slowly after him.*]

CAMERAMAN: We got to keep the shadow off her neck. You know, she's no swan. Not any more—

[*They go off.* ANNA *walks about slowly; she is uncomfortable, but doesn't quite know what to do with herself. The door to* ANDERSON'S *dressing room opens, and* ANDERSON *comes out. He is half made up for his part; he wears the medieval trousers, stockings, and slippers of the Prince; but he has on a T-shirt, and a sport coat over it. As he comes down the steps of his dressing room,* ANNA *turns toward him. He sees her, and stops.*]

ANDERSON: Why—Hello. What are *you* doing? It isn't time for lunch, is it?

ANNA [*shaking her head*]:   I just came with Mr. Freeman.

ANDERSON [*puzzled*]:   Freeman?

ANNA: Albert. He said it would be all right—

ANDERSON: Oh—Albert. Of course. Make yourself at home. [ANDERSON *comes downstage, and sits in one of the camp chairs. He has his script with him, and starts to read his lines, at first in silence, then in a low voice.* ANNA *walks in a slow circle behind him, watching him. It can be seen that to her, he is a fabulous character.*] If you say to me that a single kiss awakened you . . . that a *single* kiss awakened you . . . If you *say* to me . . . [*he grunts with annoyance*] Agh! [*he looks around, and beckons to* ANNA] You—er—what's your name? Anna . . . come here, will you, my dear, and cue me in—

ANNA [*startled*]:   Do what?

ANDERSON: Read these lines with me—[ANNA *comes hesitantly to his side. Without rising, he reaches out and pulls the other chair up for her to sit in.*] Here—sit down—[*she hesitates a moment, then does so. He hands her the script, and points to a line*] There . . . begin there—

ANNA [*first clearing her throat, then starting to read in a wooden way*]:   "I do not know who you are."

ANDERSON: "I am the shadow in the sun. I am the" . . . oh damn. Read it to me, dear.

ANNA [*very uncomfortably*]:   "I am the terror in your heart."

ANDERSON: "Terror in your heart" . . . Terror! Why terror? What the devil does it mean, anyway?

ANNA: Maybe she was afraid of him.

ANDERSON: Why? She never saw him before. He wakes her with a kiss—

ANNA [*timidly*]:   A girl might not want to be waked up like that, Mr. Anderson.

ANDERSON [*sitting back and looking at her*]:   So? Why not?

ANNA: By a total stranger—

ANDERSON [*amused*]:   Do you know, I never thought of that! Well—go on. What's the next line?

ANNA: It's yours. "If you say to me . . ."

ANDERSON: Oh yes. "If you say to me that a single kiss awakened you, you have forgotten the lost Aprils of your youth" . . . [*he stops and sighs deeply*] That's a good line: "The lost Aprils of your youth." Not bad . . . [*gently*] You wouldn't understand that, my dear.

ANNA: Anyway, it sounds beautiful—

ANDERSON [*looking at her thoughtfully*]:   No . . . April is still with you . . . How does it go?—"April that mine ears like a lover greetest" . . . The rain-sweet month, bright with birds, shy with anemones—

ANNA: Not in northern Minnesota—

ANDERSON: I suppose not.

[*The* WATCHMAN *crosses the set, from L, and stops to say a word to* ANDERSON.]

WATCHMAN: Excuse me . . . Mr. Varity was here, looking for you, Mr. Anderson—He said to tell you he'd be back.

[*He goes off, R.*]

ANDERSON: He was? . . . Hm. [*the name stirs an association of ideas; he glances thoughtfully at* ANNA] Varity . . . [*to* ANNA] Tell me, my dear . . . what's your name? Anna? That's right—Anna . . . Why isn't it Anne?

ANNA [*giving back the script*]:   I've always been Anna—

ANDERSON: Do you mind if I call you Anne?

ANNA [*trying it on for size*]:   Anne? No—why?

ANDERSON: It sounds more like you, don't you think? A little shy—and young—

158

ANNA [*in confusion*]: Why—Mr. Anderson . . . !

ANDERSON: You are. . . . Do you know Mr. Varity?

ANNA: I met him once. He ate your lunch.

ANDERSON: He spoke to me about you. He—er—he thinks you're hiding your light under a bushel.

ANNA [*in confusion*]: Under a bushel?

ANDERSON [*lightly*]: Well—in the kitchen, then.

ANNA [*weakly*]: Oh—

ANDERSON [*boldly*]: You're too attractive to be a waitress, Anne—

[ANNA *looks down in astonishment. She bites her lip— she realizes in a dim way that something—possibly opportunity, or a minor earthquake, is knocking at her door. She twists her fingers together; at last she looks up, wide-eyed, at* MR. ANDERSON.]

ANNA [*in a husky voice*]: Am I, Mr. Anderson?

ANDERSON [*set back, so to speak, on his heels*]: You— you are, you know.

ANNA [*primly*]: It was very nice of Mr. Varity to say that—

ANDERSON: I rather think he thought you should be seen about a bit . . .

ANNA [*low*]: He was making fun of me.

ANDERSON [*with meaning*]: On the contrary—

ANNA [*slowly*]: Of course, anybody wants to better themselves. But—

ANDERSON: It depends on how much they want it—is that it?

ANNA: I guess so.

ANDERSON: How much do *you* want it, Anne?

ANNA [*low*]:   I'm not sure I know what you mean—

ANDERSON [*satisfied*]:   Shall we—find out some time? [*He rises, and stands a moment looking down at her. She glances up at him, then looks away.*] Who knows? We might—both of us—better ourselves—

[*With a smile, he goes back into his dressing room. ANNA sits staring wide-eyed before her; she puts the back of her hand to her cheek. ALBERT comes in, from L.*]

ALBERT [*to the* STAND-IN, *who hasn't moved*]:   Okay, Connie . . . [CONNIE *gets up stiffly, and goes off L. At the same time, the arcs go off*] [*to* ANNA] Sorry I had to keep you waiting—

ANNA [*her mind is far away*]:   It's all right—

ALBERT [*apologizing*]:   It's sort of dull around here now —nothing much doing.

ANNA: I don't mind— [*rousing herself*] I—I better get back to work, anyway—

ALBERT: Yeah— [*looking around furtively*] Will I see you tonight—baby?

ANNA [*still slightly in shock*]:   I don't know, Albert—

ALBERT [*taken aback*]:   I thought we'd take in a picture—

ANNA: That's very nice of you, I'm sure—

ALBERT: If there's something else you'd rather do . . . We could go to the beach—

ANNA [*starting to go*]:   I'd have to think about it, Albert.

ALBERT [*bewildered*]:   Well—think about it—will you?

ANNA: I'll let you know—

[*She goes out, R.* ALBERT *stares after her: To himself, indignantly.*]

ALBERT: How do you like that? She'll let me know!

[*He turns, and as he does so,* LAVERNE *comes from her dressing room, and sees him. She is in full make-up.*]

LAVERNE: Albert—get me a stand, will you—like a good boy?

ALBERT: Sure, Miss LaVerne.

[*He goes to wings L, and brings back a lounging stand; it is a kind of vertical couch, no more than an upholstered board, against which* LAVERNE *can lean back and rest without rumpling her dress. He sets it up for her, and she nestles herself in it.*]

LAVERNE: Thank you, Albert. . . . Who were you talking to, before?

ALBERT [*uncomfortably*]:   Oh—a kid from the commissary—

LAVERNE: A kid?

ALBERT: A girl—

LAVERNE: Oh. [*thoughtfully*] She a friend of Johnny's?

ALBERT [*stupidly*]:   Johnny?

LAVERNE: John Anderson.

ALBERT [*puzzled*]:   A friend? No . . . She brings him his lunch sometimes—

LAVERNE: Rather a pretty girl, I thought—

ALBERT [*happily*]:   Did you see her?

[LAVERNE *nods.*]

LAVERNE: Yes . . . They were talking together.

ALBERT: Who?

LAVERNE: Your girl—and John—

ALBERT [*astounded*]:   They *were?*

LAVERNE: For quite a while.

ALBERT: That's funny. She didn't tell me—

LAVERNE: Almost like old friends, I'd say—

ALBERT [*trying to figure it out*]:   Humph! She was going out with me tonight.

LAVERNE: I think maybe you're going to lose your girl, Albert—

ALBERT [*shocked*]:   You do?

[LaVerne *nods. She and* ALBERT *stare at each other.* VARITY *strolls on, R. At the same time the* DIRECTOR's *voice is heard, off L.*]

DIRECTOR [*O.S.*]:   Albert! Where is that schlemiel?

[*The* WATCHMAN *appears L, and jerks his thumb backwards over his shoulder.*]

WATCHMAN: The boss wants you—

ALBERT: Okay. [*to* LaVERNE] Excuse me.

[*He starts L, then stops and looks back at* LaVERNE, *who stares at him coolly. His face takes on a look of dismal anguish, as he goes out.*]

VARITY [*coming up to* LaVERNE]:   So? Well!

LAVERNE [*lightly*]:   It's all right, grandpa. He's above the age of consent.

VARITY [*lightly*]:   He is *still* a little young for you—no?

LAVERNE [*fiercely*]:   Lay off me, will you! I don't feel like playing games. [*her eyes fill with tears; she touches her cheek below the eyes. Her voice trembles.*] You'll get my mascara running—

VARITY [*gently*]: I am not playing games, my dear. I am doing field work.

LAVERNE [*wearily*]: I don't know what you're talking about. You talk like a writer. Always aiming at something. [*holding out her hand*] Help me up, will you? [*he pulls her gently upright, off the board*] Who are you aiming at, Edgar? [*motioning to* ANDERSON'S *dressing room with her head—piteously*] Him? Why don't you leave him alone?

VARITY [*smiling, with a shrug*]: I am aiming at the sky— [*He makes a small, almost formal bow, and goes off, L. LaVerne looks after him in puzzled wonder; then thoughtfully goes toward her dressing room. ALBERT comes in from L, and crosses the stage behind her back. He goes to* ANDERSON'S *room, and knocks.*]

ANDERSON [*inside*]: Yes?

ALBERT: On the set, Mr. Anderson—

ANDERSON [*inside*]: All right . . .

[*The door opens, and* ANDERSON *appears. He is now in full make-up; the* MAKE-UP MAN *follows him down the steps; he stops, and the* MAKE-UP MAN *pats his forehead with a powder puff.*]

MAKE-UP: Just a moment—

ANDERSON: All right—take your time—

[*The* MAKE-UP MAN *pats him a little more, and stands back to look at his handiwork.*]

ALBERT: They're waiting, Mr. Anderson—

ANDERSON: They can wait— [*to* ALBERT] I hear you've got a little friend in the commissary, Albert—

ALBERT [*bitterly*]:   I *did* have—

ANDERSON [*surprised*]:   Did have? [*with lifted eyebrows*]
Sorry I brought it up.

[*He turns and starts off L, followed by the* HAIRDRESSER.
Left to himself, ALBERT *goes moodily over to the dressing
room, and looks in. He kicks the steps. He lights a cigarette, and leans against the wall of the dressing room,
brooding, balling and un-balling his fist.*]

[LAVERNE *comes out of her dressing room, followed by
her* HAIRDRESSER, *and takes her place at the ballroom
table. The* HAIRDRESSER *puts a few last touches to her
hair.* ANDERSON *comes on from L, followed by* GEORGE.
He sits down on the other chair next to LAVERNE.
GEORGE, *watching the* DIRECTOR (*O.S., L.*), *moves the
table a little to one side.*]

DIRECTOR [*O.S.*]:   All right, now . . . This is the first
time you've been by yourselves—you're awake now,
Vane . . . but you're a little afraid of it. John . . .
you think she waked up because she was ready to. You
don't figure yourself as a hero. It was fun—but you'd
rather kiss a girl with her eyes open. Vane, darling
. . . you're a little afraid. Get it?

LAVERNE: Yes, dear—

ANDERSON: Right—

DIRECTOR [*O.S.*]:   Good. Here we go.

GAFFER [*O.S.*]:   Hit your arcs—

[*The arcs go on.*]

DIRECTOR [*O.S.*]:   Let me see your faces now— [ANDER-
SON *and* LAVERNE *stare out into space with wooden*

164

expressions] A little more humble, John . . . that's it. All right—hold it . . . Roll 'em—

GEORGE [*O.S.*]:   Quiet, everybody—quiet—

MIXER'S VOICE [*O.S.*]:   Speed—

DIRECTOR [*O.S.*]:   Action!—

LAVERNE: I do not know who you are.

ANDERSON: I am the shadow in the sun. I am the terror in your heart. [LAVERNE *puts her hand to her heart.*] If you say to me that a single kiss awakened you . . .

[ALBERT, *who has been paying no attention to the scene, suddenly hits the wall of the dressing room with his fist, making a thunderous clap in the silence. At the same time he exclaims, to himself, but loudly.*]

ALBERT: Oh—nuts!

DIRECTOR [*O.S.*] [*sharply*]:   Cut!

[ANDERSON *and* LAVERNE *turn startled glances to R,* GEORGE *comes on from wings L, and looks R, angrily.*]

GEORGE: What the hell was that?

DIRECTOR [*O.S.*]:   Who did that?

[ALBERT, *who has realized too late what he has done, has been shocked into a moment of frozen horror. Now he comes forward sheepishly.*]

ALBERT: I'm sorry, George—

GEORGE: Are you crazy? You just cost us twenty feet of film. Who do you think we are? MGM?

ALBERT [*doggedly*]:   I'm sorry—

DIRECTOR [*O.S.*] [*patiently*]:   All right . . . once again —And for heaven's sake, Albert, control your feelings— whatever they are.

ALBERT [*miserably*]:   Yes, sir—

[*He and* GEORGE *go back, L;* ANDERSON *and* LAVERNE *sink back in their seats again,* ANDERSON *frowning a little,* LAVERNE *a little amused, a little excited. She thinks she knows how* ALBERT *feels. She looks at* ANDERSON, *and represses a bitter little smile.*]

LAVERNE [*out of the side of her mouth*]:   You're playing with fire, Johnny—

ANDERSON [*out of the side of his mouth*]:   Don't be silly—

DIRECTOR: All right. Once again, now.

[*A* GRIP *comes out, holds up a slate, face to the camera. Another* GRIP *snaps two blocks together in front of it.* LAVERNE *and* ANDERSON *settle in their places.*]

DIRECTOR [*O.S.*]:   Okay. Roll 'em . . .

GEORGE [*O.S.*]:   Quiet!

DIRECTOR [*O.S.*]:   Action—

[*The light begins to dim out; the voices grow fainter and fainter.*]

LAVERNE: I do not know who you are—

ANDERSON: I am the shadow in the sun. I am the mumble mumble . . .

[*The stage blacks out. It lights up again slowly on R, to show a corner of the commissary.* VARITY *is seated at a table by himself, waiting. Next to him, at another table, are* EDDIE *and* GEORGE, *eating.* ANNA *comes in with their dessert—pie and coffee.*]

ANNA [*conversationally*]:   You gentlemen were early today.

GEORGE [*short*]:   Yeah—

ANNA: Mr. Freeman isn't eating with you?

EDDIE: Not today, honey. He's making up homework—

[ANNA *looks surprised.*]

GEORGE: Yeah. Teacher kept him after school—for making a disturbance.—

ANNA [*shocked*]:   A disturbance?

EDDIE: He tried to bust up the set—

ANNA: You're kidding—

EDDIE: No—honest!

GEORGE [*to* EDDIE]:   Go on—eat your pie. We got to get back.

ANNA: Did he—did he say anything, why he did it?

EDDIE [*surprised*]:   Why he *did* it? Maybe he don't like the script. How do I know?

GEORGE: I never knew such a picture. Always trouble.

EDDIE: You said it.

GEORGE: Even the front office leaves us alone—they don't want to hear about us.

EDDIE: They'll hear about us, all right—

ANNA [*weakly*]:   Did he hurt hisself?

EDDIE [*looking up at her in surprise*]:   Who?

ANNA: Mr. Freeman—

EDDIE [*dismissing the subject*]:   Oh—him. Give us our checks, honey, will you? We're in a hurry—

GEORGE: Yeah—we got to get back—

[*She puts the two checks down on the table, and goes over to* VARITY. EDDIE *and* GEORGE *take a last bite or two, and light up cigarettes, before leaving. Meanwhile,*]

ANNA: You ready to order, Mr. Varity?

VARITY [*picking up a menu, and looking at it*]:   What do you suggest, my dear?

ANNA: The corn beef hash is all right, if you like it.

VARITY: Is it gray, or brown?

ANNA: Well—it's gray, I guess—mostly.

VARITY [*nods sadly*]:   Bring me a chicken sandwich. With a little mayonnaise on the side. And a cup of tea.

ANNA: Yes, sir. [*she starts to go.* EDDIE *and* GEORGE *get up, take their checks, and go out past her. Seeing this, she hesitates, and turns back to* VARITY *again.*] [*timidly*] Did Albert really make some trouble?

VARITY [*indifferently*]:   It was nothing—

ANNA: What did he do—

VARITY: He spoiled a take—

ANNA [*scared*]:   Will he lose his job?

VARITY: Why no—I shouldn't think so—

ANNA [*sits down suddenly, and puts her hand to her head*]:   I feel a little funny—

VARITY: Here—have some water—

ANNA: I'm all right. It's just—I thought maybe he was going to lose his job—

VARITY [*wisely*]:   I see; I see. He is a friend of yours. [ANNA *nods*] And you had a quarrel? [*she nods miserably*] And so he tried to knock a hole in a dressing room. Well—on the whole, I would say that was a credit to him.

ANNA [*sniffling a little*]:   I'd hate to have him lose his job—on my account—

VARITY: It hasn't happened yet. What was the quarrel about?

ANNA: Oh . . . It was just about going out with him—

VARITY [*nods*]:   An agreeable occupation. But not exciting—no?

ANNA [*weakly*]:   He's always been very nice—

VARITY: Of course. And you, too, have been very nice. And the air is cool, and the stars are far away . . . and the heart beats steadily, tick tock, tick tock, without scarcely losing a beat—not? [*shaking his head*] Life is full of glory and passion—but not for you. Not for Albert—

ANNA: I don't know what you're talking about.

VARITY: Of course not. You are half asleep yet—it is early for you, you are still in the Garden of Eden. Maybe, in a little while, you will wake up and see the bright sun—you will see the whole shining, glorious day, and breathe the air of flowers. Or maybe you will not see anything at all. There are women whom no passion has ever touched . . . Are you like that?

ANNA [*crying out*]:   I don't know what I'm like!

VARITY: A woman is what life makes her. She is a vessel, to be moulded by him who rouses her. That is her destiny—to be awakened by love. [*in a flat voice*] I have a note for you. [*He reaches into his pocket, and brings out an envelope. He hesitates a moment, and then, with a shrug, hands it to her across the table. She takes it, also with hesitation, and a little fearful*] I do

not pretend that this is in the best interests of the
studio—or that it dignifies my calling . . .

[ANNA *looks at him for a moment, then opens and reads
the note. It is an invitation to dine that night with* JOHN
ANDERSON. *She is startled, confused, and tempted.*]

ANNA: You know what this says?

VARITY: Naturally—

ANNA: Absolutely—I couldn't. I couldn't possibly!

VARITY [*shrugs*]: So am I to tell him no, then—you will
not dine with him?

ANNA: You know I can't . . .

VARITY: I know only what you tell me.

ANNA [*struggling*]: It's all so crazy . . .

VARITY: We have had this conversation before, I think—
[*The light begins to fade.*]

ANNA: It isn't right—

VARITY: Right—wrong—they are words in your head.

ANNA: It doesn't make sense—

VARITY [*with a careless shrug*]: Why not? He—likes
you.

ANNA: I don't have any dress—

VARITY: That can be arranged—

ANNA [*in exasperation—at her own indecision*]: Oh!

VARITY [*gently*]: Well—What shall I tell him?

ANNA [*unhappily*]: Oh dear! I oughtn't to do it—
[*The scene blacks out.*]

[*Once more the street lamp goes on at the back of the
stage.* ALBERT *stands under it, obviously waiting for
someone—*ANNA. *He smokes a cigarette nervously, look-*

*ing anxiously to right and left. A couple of young women
pass him, with sidelong glances, but he pays no attention
to them. A* MAN *goes by, and then stops.*]

MAN: Got a light, Buddy? [ALBERT *gives him a box of
matches; the* MAN *lights a cigarette, puts the matches
in his pocket, and goes off*] Thanks.

[ALBERT *looks at his watch; he holds it up under the
light. Another couple, a man and a woman, go by.* ALBERT
*throws down his cigarette, and stamps on it. Then, de-
jectedly he turns away, as the light blacks out. Further
to the L, flash bulbs go off one after another, where
photographers are taking pictures of* ANDERSON *and* ANNA
*seated together in a nightclub. (The nightclub looks not
altogether unlike the ballroom of* THE SLEEPING BEAUTY.)
*As the photographers, their pictures taken, go off, the
small lamp on the table lights up, and colored lights
wind down on* ANDERSON *and* ANNA *from above.* ANDER-
SON *is in a dinner coat,* ANNA *in a rather tasteless and
fussy gown, with a flower in her hair. She is stiff, and uncomfortable, eager, anxious and ill at ease.* ANDERSON *is
very much bored. They have finished dining, and are at
their coffee.*]

ANDERSON: They're always doing that, you know—flash-
ing lights at you—

ANNA: It made me see spots.

ANDERSON: You get used to it. Makes you jump a bit at
first . . . would you care for a drink, or something?

ANNA: Oh, no thank you.

ANDERSON: That's right—I asked you before, didn't I—

ANNA [*looking around*]:   It's wonderful enough just to be here, Mr. Anderson—

ANDERSON [*smiling bleakly*]:   Think so? You get used to that too, I'm afraid.

ANNA: I never would get used to it.

ANDERSON [*without enthusiasm*]:   No? [*his face lights up as he waves to someone offstage*] Hi—Joan—[*turning again, but by no means eagerly, to* ANNA] Wonderful girl, that.

ANNA [*eagerly*]:   I saw her in "The Heart's Desire." She was wonderful.

ANDERSON [*dully*]:   Yop. Wonderful girl. Her last picture grossed four million.

[*He sighs heavily.*]

ANNA: She must have a wonderful life.

ANDERSON [*startled*]:   Who—Joan? The only man she ever loved died in a lunatic asylum.

ANNA: Oh—

ANDERSON [*bitterly*]:   Nobody has a wonderful life. Do *you* know anybody who has a wonderful life?

ANNA: That's an awful thing to say, Mr. Anderson—

ANDERSON: You know—if you'd call me John, instead of Mr. Anderson . . .

ANNA: I couldn't do that.

ANDERSON: No? Why not? It's my name—

ANNA: It wouldn't be right, the first time like that.

ANDERSON [*teasing her a little*]:   Are there to be other times?

ANNA [*simply*]:   That's for you to say, Mr. Anderson.

ANDERSON [*coming to life momentarily*]:   Only for *me* to say?

ANNA: I always think you can tell about people when you meet them—don't you think, Mr. Anderson?

ANDERSON [*grimly*]:   John.

ANNA [*trying—but not up to it*]:   Mr. John?

ANDERSON [*giving up*]:   Never mind . . . Yes, of course.

ANNA: Of course what?

ANDERSON: What you were saying. All about . . . what *were* you saying?

ANNA: About how you can tell about people when you meet them. For instance, my Mom could always tell about anybody she met.

[*During this speech,* ANDERSON *fidgets; he glances around, and waves to several acquaintances (O.S.); he is obviously bored to death. But* ANNA *goes eagerly, warmly, and pathetically on.*]

ANDERSON [*in a half-voice—ad lib*]:   Hi, Oscar—
    Arthur—
    Louella—How are you, dear?

ANNA [*continuing regardless*]:   You know . . . whether they were people you'd want to be friends with. My Mom was wonderful that way; she was very—you know—sort of sensitive about things? My Pa wasn't so sensitive, but he had very high ideals. Once he had a chance to be on the school board, but he wouldn't accept it because there was a man on it was an atheist or something, and my Pa said if you believe in religion how can you sit down at the same table with people

who don't? I want to tell you, they taught me appreciation, because I always say life is what you make it,
and if you look for the best in people then that's what
you'll find . . . don't you think? Like [*shyly*] you
asking me out like this, and everything?

ANDERSON [*not having listened to a word of all this*]:
Sure, sure—there's Jack Gilbert over there . . .

ANNA [*looking over*]: He's very nice looking, isn't he?
Sort of a humorous face—

ANDERSON: He drew the biggest gross in history on a
P.A. in Chicago last week . . .

ANNA [*who doesn't know a P.A. from a cow's tail—staring
at* JACK GILBERT, *and nodding wisely*]: My! [*she looks
down, sighs and fusses with her coffee cup*] I always
think you can tell a . . .

ANDERSON [*suddenly*]: Oh—oh . . .

[*As* ANNA *looks up in surprise,* LAVERNE *comes in with*
VARITY. *They are ushered in by the* HEADWAITER, *who
bows them to the empty table next to* ANDERSON. ANDER-
SON *looks thunderstruck, and gloomy;* ANNA *is innocently
pleased;* VARITY *is quietly amused; and* LAVERNE *takes a
very lofty view of the whole matter—on the surface. In-
wardly, she is seething.*]

LAVERNE [*to* ANDERSON]: Good evening, Johnny. [*She
gives* ANNA *a cold stare. To the* HEADWAITER] This is
such a stuffy corner, Louis—

LOUIS: I'm sorry, Miss LaVerne—it's the only table
left—

174

[LaVerne *shrugs and sits down, as does* Varity. *He leans forward to wave to* Anderson.]

varity: Hello John. Hello, Anna—

[LaVerne *glances frostily at* Anna. Anderson *waves weakly.* Anna *nods shyly.*]

anderson: Hello, old boy—

anna: Good evening, Mr. Varity—

[*The* headwaiter *hands* Varity *and* LaVerne *menus; they disappear behind them.* Anderson *turns to* Anna.]

anderson [*conspiratorially*]:   Well!

anna [*in a stage whisper*]:   She looks older than I thought—

anderson [*with a pained look*]:   What did you expect? Margaret O'Brien? She *is* older—

anna: She's been married three times—

anderson [*gesturing*]:   Sh!

laverne [*to* headwaiter]:   I'll have a little breast of capon under glass, Louis—and asparagus vinaigrette . . .

varity: Calves brains for me—and an artichoke—

louis: Yes, Miss LaVerne. Yes, Mr. Varity—

[*He writes down the order, and starts to go.*]

varity [*calling after him*]:   And a bottle of that Rudesheimer '37 Auslese I had here last week—

louis: Yes, sir—

[*He leaves.*]

laverne [*looking around*]:   This place is going down hill fast.

ANDERSON [*realizing what is coming—to* ANNA]: You finished?

ANNA [*startled*]: Almost—

LAVERNE: You see the oddest types around here now.

ANDERSON [*calling*]: Louis . . . check please . . .

VARITY: It looks the same to me—

LAVERNE: A little blind, darling?

ANNA [*innocently to* ANDERSON]: Of course, if you're in a hurry—

ANDERSON: It's getting late—Finish your coffee, and let's go—

ANNA: All right.

[*She dutifully drains her cup.*]

LAVERNE [*clearly*]: I don't know where they come from. The kitchen, I suppose.

VARITY: Vane!

LAVERNE: Actors are funny, Edgar—did you ever notice? They take up with anybody to get a laugh.

[ANNA *puts her cup down slowly. She sits up straight, and looks woodenly ahead of her.* ANDERSON *tries to cover it up.*]

ANDERSON [*heartily—to* ANNA]: Early to bed, eh? And early to rise—

LAVERNE: Early to bed is right—

ANNA: I think maybe—we *had* better leave, Mr. Anderson—

[LOUIS *comes in with the check.* ANDERSON *signs it quickly, and he and* ANNA *rise.*]

176

LAVERNE: Doing a little baby-sitting, John?

ANDERSON: Goodnight Vane. 'Night, old boy—

ANNA [*clearly*]: Some people have a very low mind.

[*She goes out, followed by* ANDERSON. *LaVerne half rises;* VARITY *holds her back.*]

LAVERNE: What kind of a crack is that?

VARITY: Take it easy—

LAVERNE: I'll slap her ears off—

VARITY: Oh stop it! Do you want to be thrown out of here?

LAVERNE: What do *I* care?

VARITY: The studio cares. That would be a fine scandal —"Film star and waitress tangle over actor" . . .

LAVERNE [*letting herself be pulled back*]: What a low heel he is—

VARITY: My dear child—What should he be? Sir Galahad? Prince Albert? Be reasonable; you are no Queen Victoria.

LAVERNE: I should have pasted her—I should have pasted both of them—

VARITY: For what? Do you think he has been enjoying himself? This is no meeting of minds, my pet. The poor fellow is bored to death already.

LAVERNE [*piteously*]: You think so?

VARITY: Of course. I knew he would be. All evening he has been waiting for her to ask him for his autograph— No, no, he is not happy—believe me.

LAVERNE: I hope he's burning in Hell.

VARITY: What he is doing is not important.

LAVERNE [*belligerently*]:   What do you mean, it's not important?

VARITY: To you, maybe—but not to me. It is the girl that interests me—the unawakened Eve.

LAVERNE: You're a rotten devil, Edgar—

VARITY: Sure, sure. But not the way you think. And I will tell you something else. You think he has taken her home with him? No. He has sent her home in a taxi. You will find him in the bar, drinking . . . by himself, out of ennui.

[LaVERNE *looks at* EDGAR *reflectively. Then she leans far out over the table, and looks off to R. Her face relaxes, and she smiles; she settles herself back with a sigh.*]

LAVERNE: You're a pretty clever guy, darling—

VARITY: Was I right?

[LaVERNE *nods happily. The stage blacks out. A light picks up a spot further to the R. It shows—one after another—two bars, back to back; one is in the nightclub, the other in a saloon. Sitting at the nightclub bar, is* ANDERSON, *alone, moodily drinking a scotch and soda. As he fades out, the other bar comes to light; there sits* ALBERT, *also alone, and equally glum, drinking a beer. The* MILKMAN *now walks across the stage, C, and disappears. The two bars black out, and the stage gradually lightens, to show its customary daylight face; the ballroom set is as before, with* GEORGE *and* WARDROBE *bending over the table, studying several medieval dresses which are laid out for them.*]

WARDROBE: This is as near to fifteenth century stuff as we could find, George.

GEORGE: They'll do. We want eight of them, for background—

WARDROBE: Okay—

GEORGE: Leave one of them here, till I show the boss—

WARDROBE: Will do.

[*He gathers up all but one of the dresses and goes off.*]

GEORGE [*calling*]: Hey—Albert—

[ALBERT *comes in from L, passing* WARDROBE.]

ALBERT: Yeah?

GEORGE: Keep an eye on this, will you? I want the boss to see it.

ALBERT: Will do—

GEORGE [*irritably*]: What is that, will do, will do? We're not making Battleground, for cripe's sake!

ALBERT [*dejectedly*]: Yes, sir—

GEORGE: And look—cheer up, will you? You're giving me the willies. Do you think a fellow never got stood up by a dame before? It happens all the time.

ALBERT: That don't make *me* feel better.

GEORGE: All right—so this is an extra special dish. Only, we happen to be making a picture. We already lost a hundred grand on it, when VARITY stepped out, and the boss had to take over. That isn't peanuts, kid. So one more crack out of you when we're on a take, and you go back to the messengers.

ALBERT: Yes, sir—

GEORGE: Okay, baby—Just keep your eye on this dress,

and your nose clean, and your mouth shut— [*he starts to go off, R. After a few steps, he turns, and adds*] And leave the girls alone—

ALBERT [*miserably*]: Aw . . . [GEORGE *goes, and* ALBERT *sits down in dejection beside the table. He whistles, dolefully, the same tune we heard so gaily piped in Act I.* ANNA *comes in from R, in her apron, with a tray for* ANDERSON. *She goes to the dressing room and knocks, but there is no answer. Non-plussed, she knocks again, then turns slowly away.* ALBERT, *who has seen her, and tried to act as though he hadn't, speaks to her over his shoulder.*] Your boyfriend's stepped out.

ANNA [*coldly*]: I'm sure I don't know what you mean by that remark, Mr. Freeman—

ALBERT [*darkly*]: You know what I mean, all right.

ANNA: I don't know what gives you the right to make a remark like that about a gentleman who's never been anything but a gentleman to me—

ALBERT: Where were you last night—?

ANNA [*coldly*]: I was taken to dinner in a very public place where I saw a lot of people I knew.

ALBERT: Yeah. And afterwards?

ANNA: Afterwards, I went home, and anyway I don't see what right you have to ask me questions. Where were *you?*

ALBERT [*flabbergasted*]: *Me?*

ANNA: Yes, you—So long as you seem to think you have the right to ask—

[*She comes to the table, and puts down her tray.*]

ALBERT: I was waiting for you—that's where *I* was. And then I went to a—place, and got stinking.

ANNA [*in a rush of pity, remorse, outraged virtue, and pleased surprise at finding herself such a femme fatale*] Oh Albert!

ALBERT [*sullenly*]:   Well—what did you expect me to do—? Join the Boy Scouts?

ANNA: Oh Albert—you take everything so seriously!

ALBERT: I thought you liked serious people—

ANNA: I do. Only—you can get *too* serious, Albert. I mean—just because I go out with you and—let you— you know—kiss me once or twice—that doesn't mean I can't go out to dinner in a public place with a very distinguished gentleman when he asks me . . . does it? A woman has got to better herself in every way, Albert, on account of that is her destiny.

ALBERT: Holy Cow.

ANNA: And anyway, if you want to know, I went right home after dinner. So you see!

ALBERT [*grudgingly*]:   Well—that's something, anyhow —But just the same—he isn't fooling *me* any! I know what he's after.

ANNA: Oh Albert! Really! You ought to be ashamed. I think you've got a low mind! [*she sees the dress on the table, and touches it*] What's that for?

ALBERT: Some extra—All right, so I got a low mind. But I know what I know—

ANNA: If I'm not worrying, why should you? You

haven't a thing to worry about—and anyway, a gentleman like that respects a person . . . [*holding the dress
up*] It's pretty . . . all that stuff. It's silk—

ALBERT: Sure. [*she holds it up against her shoulders*]
You'd look good in it, kid—

ANNA [*eagerly*]: Would I?—I wish I could see how it
looks . . . could I try it on once, do you think, Albert?

ALBERT [*doubtfully*]: Gee, baby—if anybody came—

ANNA: No one would see me—

ALBERT [*looking around*]: It'd be as much as my life
was worth—

ANNA: I could say I was an extra—

ALBERT: Gee, kid, I don't know—

ANNA: Please, Albert—

ALBERT: Well . . . just for a minute, see . . . to look
at. Skip into one of those dressing rooms—don't take
long, now. [*as she goes eagerly off with the dress, L*]
And if anybody comes, you just say you're from wardrobe—

[*He looks anxiously around the stage, starts to light a
cigarette, then sees the tray, picks it up, and starts for
ANDERSON's dressing room. As he gets to the step, ANDER-
SON comes briskly on from R. He is in an ordinary business suit.*]

ANDERSON: Hello, there . . . that for me?

ALBERT [*confused*]: Yes, sir—It's your lunch was left
here—

ANDERSON [*looks at it*]: I see. Well—take it back, will

you—like a good fellow? And tell them to send me a
pot of hot soup—and a chop, instead—

ALBERT [*anxiously*]: Well, gee, Mr. Anderson, I . . .
George told me . . . you know, I'm supposed to stay
here—

ANDERSON: That's all right. Tell George I sent you—

ALBERT: But—I've got to—

ANDERSON: They won't be back here for over an hour
yet. They've gone to look at a set-up on Lot 2. Be a
good fellow—run it up for me—

ALBERT [*swallowing miserably*]: W-what is it you want?

ANDERSON: Just a pot of hot soup—and a chop—

ALBERT [*sighing heavily*]: Okay—

[*He goes heavily off, R. ANDERSON starts into his dressing
room, then turns back, and goes slowly toward the table.
He whistles rather tunelessly. He stops in front of the
table, and says half to himself, as though trying it out—*]

ANDERSON: "I am the shadow in the sun . . . I am the
terror in your heart". . . [*suddenly breaking into
mimicry of the night before*] Do *you* know anybody
who has a wonderful life? [*He hits the table irritably,
and turns away. As he starts moodily toward his dressing room, ANNA comes around the corner of the set, C.
She is in the medieval gown, and looks really lovely.
The gown is full at the skirt, and very bare at the
shoulder. She stops in dismay when she sees ANDER-
SON.*] [*startled*] Hello! Who are you? [*coming closer*]
Anne? By jove—what are *you* doing in that?

183

ANNA [*scared*]:   I was just trying it on—I'll take it off—
[*She half turns to flee, but he puts up a hand to stop her.*]

ANDERSON: Please—I wouldn't dream of it. Don't take
it off. [*he goes up to her, and turns her around to face
him. She is embarrassed and miserable.*] [*slowly, with
relish*] Let me look at you . . . I say, you're quite
lovely . . . I didn't realize . . .

ANNA [*keeping her head bent*]:   Please—

ANDERSON [*tilting her face up with a finger under her
chin*]:   Let me see you . . . charming. I didn't know
your eyes were so blue . . . like April—

ANNA [*still expostulating, but her heart is beating*]:
Honest, Mr. Anderson—

ANDERSON [*softly*]:   John . . . I was lonely last night—
after you left me—

ANNA [*half-whispering*]:   Were you?

ANDERSON: The moon was shining, and there was a
scent of jasmine over everything; and sweet mock
orange; and a little bitter smell of eucalyptus. It makes
a man lonely—for the lost Aprils, Anne . . . you have
a very sweet mouth—

ANNA [*dizzily—she is beginning to be a little afraid—
and a little excited, too*]:   Really?

ANDERSON [*he starts to draw her toward his dressing
room*]:   You have so much to give . . . so much
youth . . .

ANNA [*holding back*]:   I don't know—

184

ANDERSON: So much beauty, Anne. There's comfort in beauty, it holds time back . . . like this.

[*He stoops to kiss her gently. She stands transfixed.*]

ANNA [*in a whisper*]:   It's like in the movies—

ANDERSON [*drawing her toward the dressing room*]: Beauty won't last forever—it's meant for now. For the living, Anne . . . for the lonely and the hungry . . . come—

ANNA: Oh, please—we mustn't—

ANDERSON: How else can we forget the dark? Or the bright, empty day . . . ? Give me a little of your youth, Anne—for the long journey through autumn—

ANNA: That was from a picture—

ANDERSON: But this wasn't. [*he takes her in his arms, and kisses her. She sways against him; she seems overborne*] [*triumphantly*] Anne!

ANNA [*moaning*]:   It isn't right!

[*He leads her up the stairs of his dressing room, and closes the door. A moment goes by. Then* ALBERT *comes on, R. He crosses the stage quickly.*]

ALBERT: Anna . . . Anna? [*he stops a moment at the table, and looks around*] Anna?

[*Uncertain, troubled, he goes off L. Another moment goes by, then, from inside the dressing room comes the sound of a girl's low sobbing, and*

THE CURTAIN FALLS

ACT III

[*The curtain goes up on a dark stage.* ALBERT *is heard whistling dolefully. Then* GEORGE *is heard calling.*]

GEORGE'S VOICE: Albert—Hey—Albert—
[*The lights go on. The set is as it was in the first act.* GEORGE, EDDIE, *the* GAFFER, *and the* WATCHMAN *are playing bridge, C, on the table from Act II.*]

GEORGE: One diamond.

EDDIE: What kind of a bid is that?

GEORGE: Never mind—Hey, Albert!

EDDIE: Pass—

GAFFER: Three diamonds—

EDDIE: Aw, for Pete's sake—

WATCHMAN: Can't do it. Pass—

GEORGE: Pass—

[ALBERT *comes on, L. He is subdued.*]

ALBERT: You call me, George?

GEORGE: Yah. On account of you are never where I expect you to be. [*they start to play*] Where are the new pages?

ALBERT: Script has them—

GEORGE: What's the matter?

186

ALBERT: They're waiting for an okay from the Breen office—

GEORGE: How do you like that? We change a couple of lines of dialogue, and we got censorship troubles. [*playing out a card*] Let's have the queen.

ALBERT [*looking over* EDDIE's *shoulder*]: I'd hold it—

EDDIE: Let me play my own game, will you? [*throwing down a card*] Sure—The old man sends my script to Joplin, Missouri, and if in two weeks there's no rise in juvenile delinquency, we're in.

WATCHMAN: How come they can make those new gangster pictures all the time?

EDDIE: That's a peculiarity of the country, Pop. You take a hood can climb into a window and stick up a house, and maybe beat the householder over the head with a forty-five, and even mess around a little with his wife—and what does he get? Probation—and maybe his driving license taken away from him. On account of he's only doing his natural business. But the householder who pops off at him with a twenty-two—he's liable to get ten years. They figure he should have called the police. He's an amateur, see?

GEORGE: The rest are good. [*he lays down his hand, and starts figuring the score*] That's a five rubber— [EDDIE *and the* WATCHMAN *both throw down a quarter, which* GEORGE *and the* GAFFER *pocket. They all rise, and go off, L*] [*as they go off, to* ALBERT] Go on back to script, and tell 'em we want those pink pages—

187

ALBERT: Okay—

GAFFER: What do you work in this business for, Eddie?
A smart guy like you?

EDDIE: Aw—my kids like to think I have lunch every
day with Esther Williams—

[*They exit. As they do so, a* GRIP *trundles a parallel across
the stage from R, leaves it near the wings, and follows
them off, L.* VARITY *and* ANDERSON *stroll in from R. They
are chatting;* ANDERSON *wears his sport jacket over his
costume.*]

ANDERSON: Well—it's a smash hit. He says Tandy's
terrific. She carries the whole play.

VARITY [*shrugs*]: Why not? She's an actress—

ANDERSON: You know—we had her under contract here.
We let her go.

VARITY [*drily*]: Naturally—She would change all the
values in the industry.

[ANDERSON *sits down on one of the two camp chairs, R,
Center.*]

ANDERSON: Got a minute?

[VARITY *nods, and sits down beside him.*]

VARITY: What's on your mind?

ANDERSON [*looks studiedly at his nails*]: I'm in a bit of
a jam, old boy—

VARITY [*lifting his eyebrows*]: Again?

ANDERSON: Oh—nothing very much . . . Nothing serious. It's just that that kid from the commissary might
want to make a little trouble for me—

VARITY: Nothing serious, you say?

ANDERSON:　There were no promises, old boy—I didn't commit myself to anything.

VARITY:　Hm. [*he shakes his head soberly*] Strange.

ANDERSON [*unhappily*]:　You know how those things happen—

VARITY [*slowly*]:　I have seen the young lady this morning, John. She served me breakfast—

ANDERSON:　How did she seem?

VARITY:　That is what puzzles me. She seemed—just as usual, if you ask me.

ANDERSON [*startled*]:　She did?

VARITY:　The same somewhat vacant manner—a little more so, perhaps—

ANDERSON [*puzzled, but relieved*]:　Well—that's good, old boy—

VARITY:　Ah—but is it? A woman is like a trout, John—she moves about in a sub-aqueous world of her own. When she does not show herself, you do not know what she is up to.

ANDERSON [*sulkily*]:　What did you expect her to do? Light up like a pin ball machine?

VARITY [*gravely*]:　Yes—I did. But this girl fools me. [*he scratches his head ruefully*] Maybe I am wrong about her.

ANDERSON:　It's upsetting, old boy. I wish you'd never started it—

VARITY:　I? I started it?

ANDERSON [*defensively*]:　Well . . . you put the idea into my head.

VARITY [*smiling a little bitterly, and rising*]: Always
the director to put the ideas in people's heads. Sit
here, sit there, think this, think that, now you are in
love, now you are not, now you are happy, now you
are sad . . . I am going back to RKO, to my a-a-a-a-a,
and my tommy guns.

[*He turns away.*]

ANDERSON [*also rising*]: Not mad, are you, old boy?

VARITY [*wearily*]: Mad? No. I am not mad. I am tired
of my own subtlety, is all— [*he looks around, and then
up, towards Heaven*] Sometimes I think He out-
maneuvers me—

[*Shaking his head, he goes.* ANDERSON *looks after him in
surprise, then goes into his own dressing room, and closes
the door. A* GRIP *comes in front, and takes away the
table and the chairs around it.* GEORGE *comes in, L, crossing him, and calls.*]

GEORGE: Bring your dollies down— [*two* GRIPS *comes in
from L, and lay down two boards (a runway or dolly,
for the camera).* GEORGE *watches them*] A little to the
left, I think. [*calling*] How far back you want to go,
Chief?

DIRECTOR [*O.S.*]: That's enough—

[*The back of a camera truck now rolls out onto the
dollies, pushed by two members of the camera crew. A*
SOUND MAN *rolls in his mike boom; a* GRIP *sets up another
arc. Everything is aimed at a scene offstage, to L. A* GRIP
attaches a large electric cable to the camera truck. A

*member of the camera crew makes a chalk mark on one
of the dollies, by the rear wheel.*]

CREW MEMBER: Number one. [GEORGE *watches*]

CAMERAMAN [*O.S.*]:   Bring her forward— [*the* CAMERA
  CREW *pushes the camera truck forward a foot or two,
  toward the wings.*] Okay. Mark two.

[*The* CREW MEMBER *makes a chalk mark on the dolly. The
crew files off, L. Meanwhile,* ANNA *has come on from R.
She walks slowly across the stage, toward the camera
truck. She is very quiet—withdrawn—more asleep, it almost seems, than ever. As the men go out, she touches*
GEORGE *timidly on the arm.*]

ANNA: Excuse me—is Albert here?

GEORGE [*turning*]:   Albert? . . . Oh—hello.

ANNA [*quietly*]:   Hello.

GEORGE [*amiably*]:   Why Albert, sweetheart? Why not
  somebody your own size?

ANNA [*half turns away; she smiles without gaity, a small,
  bleak, polite smile*]:   I thought maybe he was here—

GEORGE: He's here, I guess— [*calling*] Hey—Albert . . .
  Oh, that's right, I sent him over to script. He'll be back.
  Sit down and wait, if you like—

ANNA: Thanks.

[*She turns slowly toward the center of the stage.* GEORGE
looks after her with relish.]

GEORGE: Albert got an option on you, baby?—or what?

ANNA [*with quiet bitterness*]:   Nobody's got an option
  on me.

GEORGE: Okay—don't get sore. I was just asking.

ANNA [*dully*]:   I'm not sore—

GEORGE [*reassuringly*]:   You can't blame a guy for asking—

ANNA: I just thought maybe I could see Albert a minute, if you don't mind—

GEORGE: Why would I mind? Make yourself comfortable—

[*He waves his hand carelessly, and goes off, L. She looks after him dully; she glances around the set. She stares at* ANDERSON'S *dressing room, with a cold, hard look; and moves slowly and icily away from it, toward R. As she does so,* ALBERT *comes in, holding a number of pink typewritten pages in his hand. He stops when he sees* ANNA; *she looks at him quietly.*]

ALBERT [*self-conscious ly*]:   Hi ya.

ANNA [*quietly*]:   Hello, Albert—

[PROPS *comes in quickly, R. He carries a jeweled dagger in his hand.*]

PROPS: Hey, Albert . . . do me a favor, will you? Here —take this. [*he gives* ALBERT *the dagger*] I'm in a hurry—

ALBERT [*looking at the dagger in surprise*]:   Who's it for?

PROPS [*leaving*]:   For Mr. Anderson—give it to him, will you?

[*He goes out, R.*]

ALBERT [*calling back*]:   Okay . . . [*he turns and faces* ANNA] Hi ya.

ᴀɴɴᴀ:　I was looking for you, Albert—

ᴀʟʙᴇʀᴛ [*a little pleased, but still self-conscious*]:　Yeah?
Well . . . What's on your mind . . . Anna?

ᴀɴɴᴀ:　I wanted to apologize for yesterday, Albert. For
not waiting for you. [*she takes a breath, and makes
the plunge*] I had to go back to work—

ᴀʟʙᴇʀᴛ [*relieved and aggrieved all at once*]:　Well, Gee,
kid—that's all right. Only—you got me in dutch, did
you know that?

ᴀɴɴᴀ:　I'm sorry, Albert.

ᴀʟʙᴇʀᴛ:　Yeah—you got the dress all mussed up . . . I
didn't even know where you put it, till I found it over
in a corner somewhere. Jeez, George was fit to be tied
. . . What happened to you, honey?

ᴀɴɴᴀ:　I—I was just sort of—you know—trying it on,
and—then it got late—Where were you?

ᴀʟʙᴇʀᴛ [*motioning toward* ᴀɴᴅᴇʀsᴏɴ's *dressing room*]:
The emperor here sent me out for something—

ᴀɴɴᴀ:　Did he? . . . [*with a catch in her voice*] That's
funny . . .

ᴀʟʙᴇʀᴛ:　Yeah—when I came back, you'd gone. I tried
to reach you last night, and you don't answer . . .
What's so funny?

ᴀɴɴᴀ [*dully*]:　Nothing, I guess. I wish I'd been home
when you phoned—

ᴀʟʙᴇʀᴛ [*mollified*]:　Yeah—I thought we'd take in a
picture. Where were you?

ᴀɴɴᴀ:　I went down to the beach by myself. And looked
at the water.

ALBERT: No kidding!

ANNA: That's what I did.

ALBERT: I wish I'd known it—

ANNA: A girl has to think things out sometimes, Albert. I mean, for herself. I think now maybe I was wrong about a certain thing . . . And I thought I'd tell you.

ALBERT [*mystified*]:   Yeah? Well—that's swell.

ANNA: I mean—Like finding out about your destiny . . . and the kind of person you are. Because maybe you think it'll be—you know—something wonderful, like you might want to find out about yourself . . . and then it just—you know—isn't.

ALBERT [*more mystified than ever*]:   Uh—huh.

ANNA: I just—wanted you to know.

ALBERT: Well—I don't know just what you mean—but whatever it is, it's okay with me. Only—how come you got that dress so mussed up yesterday? It put me on a spot, kid. George was going to take my head off. He was foaming!

ANNA [*frightened*]:   I'm—sorry, Albert—

ALBERT: It don't matter—but I can't figure it out. What were you doing?

ANNA [*with difficulty*]:   I . . . It must have been when I took it off—

ALBERT [*slowly*]:   Uh—huh. [*rather anxiously*] Well—where were you when you took it off?

ANNA: In a dressing room.

ALBERT: Did anybody see you? [ANNA *shakes her head, with a rather desperate expression*] Are you sure,

baby? [ANNA *nods*] Because—I could lose my job.
You know that. I told George it must have got mussed
up by some grip sitting on it . . . but I don't know,
he . . .

[ANDERSON *comes out of his dressing room, holding his
script, and starts across to L.*]

ANDERSON: Oh—Eddie . . . have you got a minute?
[*he suddenly notices* ANNA, *and turns. To* ANNA—]
Hello darling . . . I'll be right back. Don't go away—
[*he goes on toward L, then stops and turns back*] By
the way. I spoke to the director about you— [ANNA
*makes a frightened gesture, as though to beg him to
stop.* ALBERT *pricks up his ears*] He said he'd like to
see you— [ANNA *looks at* ALBERT, *piteously, for a
moment, and then looks away.* ALBERT *stares at* ANDER-
SON] In that same dress—you know? The one off the
shoulders—

[*He nods, and goes off L.*]

[ANNA *stands frozen, watching him go off. The pink
papers fall from* ALBERT's *hand; he stoops awkwardly to
pick them up. He doesn't look at* ANNA.]

ALBERT: Why does he call you darling? [ANNA *doesn't
speak. She just shakes her head. Her world is tumbling
down around her, and her throat is too tight*] Nobody
saw you, huh? The dress from wardrobe, off the shoulders . . . [*he glances at* ANDERSON's *dressing room*]
You took it off in a dressing room, so that's why it got
mussed up . . . huh? I think I can figure it. [*bitterly,
his voice breaking*] Why did you give me all that crap?

ANNA [*in a tight, weak voice*]:   I—didn't mean to—

ALBERT [*nearly weeping*]:   Okay—you didn't mean to.
Well—why did you? [*violently*] What are you doing?
Making a fool out of me?

[ANNA *shakes her head. Two tears run down her cheeks.
She turns, and starts slowly, almost mechanically, off, R.
ALBERT holds the knife and the papers in his hands; he
turns miserably away, as the* WATCHMAN *comes on from
R., crossing* ANNA. *The* WATCHMAN *looks at her curiously as she goes by.* GEORGE *comes on from L; he goes
up to* ALBERT, *who seems in a daze.*]

GEORGE: You got the script, kid? Jeez, you took forever!
Let's have it— [ALBERT *hands the pages to him, and
he hurries off L with them*] They've been going
crazy—

[*Meanwhile, the* WATCHMAN *has come down C, and
seated himself by the telephone.* ALBERT *turns back, and
still holding the dagger, goes and leans dejectedly against
the table. The* CAMERA CREW *comes on, L; they take their
positions on the camera truck; the* SOUND MAN *mounts
his boom;* GRIPS *come out, and stand about, looking back,
offstage, at the scene which is about to be rehearsed.*]

GAFFER [*O.S.*]:   Hit your arcs—

[*The arcs go on, making a pool of light offstage. The*
WATCHMAN *opens a newspaper—begins to read;* ALBERT
*plays moodily with the dagger, lifting it up out of its
sheath, and trying the edge with his thumb.*]

DIRECTOR'S VOICE [*O.S.*]:   This is a camera rehearsal.
Take your places . . . you're not quite at the chalk

mark, dear . . . That's better. Now you turn around, dear . . . that's right—face away from me . . . camera . . . [*the* GRIPS *push the camera forward to mark two, the* SOUND MAN *extends his boom*] That all right, Joe?

CAMERAMAN [*O.S.*]:   Okay—I guess . . .

DIRECTOR [*O.S.*]:   Let's try it again . . .

[*The crew push the camera back. They watch for a while, and then push it forward. The* SOUND MAN *extends his boom. Meanwhile:*]

ALBERT [*moodily*]:   This dagger's sharp all right. You'd think they wouldn't use a real knife, like that.

WATCHMAN: Be glad there's something real around here—

ALBERT: Yes, I guess so. Nothing else is—

WATCHMAN: Things didn't turn out so good, huh?

ALBERT [*looking at the knife*]:   Somebody could cut hisself with this—

WATCHMAN: You'd better stop playing with it, kid.

ALBERT: What is it about a girl, Pop, you think she couldn't do anything—you know—that wasn't right on the line?—and some ham comes along, and right away she's a tramp.

WATCHMAN: Put the knife away, kid, before you hurt yourself—

ALBERT: Don't worry—I'm not going to hurt myself—

DIRECTOR [*O.S.*]:   All right, everybody . . . we'll shoot this after lunch . . .

GAFFER: Kill your arcs— [*the arcs go off*]

GEORGE: Break for lunch. One hour. [*the crew wanders off, some to L, others crossing stage to R. GEORGE and EDDIE go off, R*] What do you like in the fifth, Eddie?

EDDIE: Man O'War—

GEORGE: Oh sure. Come on—be serious—

EDDIE: Rose Velvet, then—

GEORGE: She carries too much weight—

EDDIE: You asked me, didn't you? And I told you.

GEORGE: Okay—okay—

[*They go off. The* WATCHMAN *also goes off.* ANDERSON *and* LaVERNE *come on, L.* LaVERNE *walks coldly, with her nose in the air.* ANDERSON *is a little sheepish.*]

ANDERSON: After all, old girl—you could look at me when we do a scene. I mean—it's a little embarrassing to have you keep staring at my teeth—

LAVERNE [*coldly*]: "The better to bite you with, my dear"—

ANDERSON: Be reasonable, will you?

LAVERNE: There are too many lost Aprils in your life, Johnny. You're—drenched in them. I'm going to lunch.

ANDERSON [*as she goes off, R*]: What about dinner tonight?

LAVERNE [*looking back, maliciously*]: It still looks too much like rain, Johnny.

[ANDERSON *looks after her. Then he turns, and goes to his dressing room.* ALBERT *makes a gesture, as though to get up; he half holds out the knife to him, but* ANDERSON *doesn't notice him, and* ALBERT *sinks back again.* ALBERT *is now alone on the stage. He plays moodily with the knife.*]

ALBERT [*to himself*]:   Just a tramp.

[*The light grows dimmer on the stage. At the same time, a strange, and rather ominous cloud effect is noticed on the cyclorama, while a gentle, rosy glow illuminates the wings, offstage, L.*]

DIRECTOR'S VOICE [*O.S.*] [*gently*]:   Albert . . .

[ALBERT *does not hear. His fingers tighten on the knife; he half raises it, as though to strike something.*]

ALBERT: A tramp.

DIRECTOR [*O.S.*]:   Albert—

[ALBERT *looks up uncertainly.*]

ALBERT: Yes? . . . Somebody call me?

DIRECTOR [*O.S.*]:   I did, Albert—

ALBERT: Oh . . . yes sir? [*starting up*] Did you want me?

DIRECTOR: Don't move . . . don't move. I don't want anything—I'm just resting here.

ALBERT [*sitting back—uncomfortably*]:   Yes sir—

DIRECTOR: It was a tiring morning, Albert. "And on the Seventh Day, He rested". . . How are things with you?

ALBERT: They're all right, I guess—

DIRECTOR: You guess . . . ? Well, that's right; one should never be too sure—in this business. It's like life . . . The rewards are few—and uncertain. Sometimes I wonder why I bother to make pictures—

ALBERT: Yes sir.

DIRECTOR: But then, suddenly, there is a moment of pure beauty—or of joy—and then I know . . . [*he sighs*] Have you ever had such moments in your life, Albert?

ALBERT: No sir—

DIRECTOR [*musingly*]: No—I suppose not. But you will have other moments, Albert. When suddenly life takes you to itself . . . Well—I am going to nap for a little while—

ALBERT: Yes, sir—

DIRECTOR: There is some good in everything, Albert. Even this shoddy business we are in . . .

ALBERT [*shaking his head*]: I don't believe it.

DIRECTOR [*sleepily*]: Tell them not to disturb me. And Albert—

ALBERT: Yes, sir?

DIRECTOR: Put the knife away.

[ALBERT *sits staring ahead of him, as the glow at L fades out, and the stage darkens a little. At last he rouses himself.*]

ALBERT [*quietly and ominously*]: Yes, sir. I'll put it where it belongs—

[*He gets up and goes slowly towards* ANDERSON's *dressing room. He mounts the steps, and hesitates; then takes a deep breath, opens the door, and steps inside, closing the door behind him. The* WATCHMAN *strolls on from R. There is a moment of silence. Then, from the dressing room—*]

ANDERSON'S VOICE [*raised in fright*]:   Here—put that down—! What do you want? Hey! Somebody! Quit it! Pop! George! Get him out of here! [*The* WATCHMAN *rushes to the dressing room. The* GAFFER *and several* GRIPS *run in from R, and all crowd into the dressing room*] Get him out of here!

[*The stage blacks out.*]

[*The stage lights up at R, to show a corner of the commissary. The two tables are empty, the diners are gone;* ANNA *and the other waitress are clearing up.*]

WAITRESS: I don't like to say anything, dearie, but I couldn't help overhearing my gentlemen—they was talking about this young man—you know—Albert? I believe you've made his acquaintance. [ANNA *stands still as stone*] Well . . . you know how he spoiled a take the other day? My gentlemen were fit to be tied . . . only now he's in real trouble. It seems he went after somebody with a knife. Tst, tst . . . You know, he's the brooding type. [*she sighs heavily*] I feel sorry for him, what they'll do to him now. If it was the chef, the one that's always pinching my fanny when I go by —I wish he'd get it!

[*She gathers up her dishes and goes off.*]

[ANNA *stands for a moment as though frozen. Then she starts to gather her dishes, very quietly. But suddenly, she puts them down, and with fumbling fingers, begins to untie her apron. The scene blacks out. The telephone rings on the set, in the darkness.*]

WATCHMAN'S VOICE: Stage five . . . Yes? Miss La-

Verne's not here . . . I don't know—the set has closed down for the day. No—you'll have to ask the front office about that, ma'am—

[*He clicks the phone off. The stage lights up at L, to show a corner of a terrace against the cyclorama of the city. Lying on a chaise, under an umbrella, is* ANDERSON; LAVERNE *sits on a chair beside him.*]

ANDERSON: I could have taken care of it all right—but you know, I didn't want to hurt the boy—

LAVERNE: What did he do? Try to cut you?

ANDERSON [*uncomfortably*]:   To tell you the truth, I don't quite know . . . You know, when a fellow comes at you—like that . . .

LAVERNE: Poor kid . . . I feel sorry for him. I suppose he'll get the works.

ANDERSON [*negligently*]:   I suppose so—

LAVERNE: I told you you were playing with fire, Johnny—

ANDERSON: You know, old girl—you rather make me feel like a salamander—

LAVERNE: The pitcher that goes too often to the well—

ANDERSON: Am I really an old crock, Vane?

LAVERNE [*biting her lip*]:   You know, Johnny—you don't deserve to have me answer that—

ANDERSON [*reaching for her hand*]:   Am I—darling?

LAVERNE: Oh Johnny—you *are* a lizard! [*she bends to kiss him, lightly, and then sits up again*] Why don't we go away for a while. To Mexico—

ANDERSON [*mechanically*]:   Me—hi—co—

LAVERNE: Me—hi—co . . . I know. It's just a place.
And we've done everything in the world . . . don't
let's start that again.

ANDERSON: No . . . I guess after a while you just run
out of starts, darling.

LAVERNE [*anxiously*]: And then—?

ANDERSON [*thoughtfully*]: And then . . . why, I guess
you just keep on going, old girl—

LAVERNE: Looking for April still?

ANDERSON [*gently*]: Summer's not such a bad season,
you know—

LAVERNE: Thank you, Johnny . . . I thought maybe
you were going to say Autumn—

ANDERSON: Don't be unreasonable, darling . . .

[*He draws her down to him, as the stage darkens out. A
light goes on, C, to show* ALBERT *sitting defiantly in front
of the* WATCHMAN, EDDIE, *the* GAFFER, GEORGE *and two
more policemen. They ring him in, curiously.*]

GEORGE: Come on, kid—spill it. What were you trying
to do?

[ALBERT *is sullenly silent.*]

WATCHMAN: You'd better tell us, Albert—

GEORGE: Yeah—After all, we're your friends, kid—

ALBERT: Nobody's my friends—

EDDIE [*to* GEORGE]: You know, people go berserk sometimes, for no reason. Like that fellow over at Pismo
beach, ripped up that woman with a can opener. You
know, one of those new things, that go around? He'd
never seen her before . . . a perfect stranger. It seems

he couldn't get the thing to work—it wouldn't open anything. So he goes crazy, and tries it on this woman.

GAFFER: Yeah. We got one of those. It all depends on how you put the can in—

GEORGE: The hell with that. Albert—come on—spill it. What were you trying to do?

[ALBERT *is silent. As they stare at him,* VARITY *comes sauntering in from R. He is surprised, and comes over to them.*]

VARITY: Hello . . . What is this? Story conference?

GEORGE: No, sir . . . A little trouble—

VARITY: With our young friend? What's the matter?

GEORGE: Oh—he had a knife . . . We had to take it away from him—

VARITY: Oh—

GEORGE: So, now he won't talk—

WATCHMAN: He won't talk—

VARITY: Tst . . . That's too bad . . . was anyone hurt?

GEORGE: Well—they might have been—

VARITY: What's the matter, Albert? Did you also eat of the forbidden fruit?

ALBERT: Everything's lies.

EDDIE: Sure, everything's lies, kid. Everybody lies in the movies. It's part of the business. So what?

VARITY: This is not just a matter of business, I think . . . This is perhaps more a matter of the heart. That small reality which in the business we do not bother about . . . Gentlemen, there are too many of you

here; you are like an inquisition. After all, if there was
no one hurt . . .

GEORGE: We got to protect the picture.

GAFFER: Why don't you just fire him?

GEORGE [*scornfully*]:   Yeah—So he goes to the newspapers. Suppose he's *got* a real beef? So we get a lot
of adverse publicity. You got to find out what he's got.

EDDIE: Maybe he don't like actors—

VARITY: Gentlemen . . . I have a suggestion: I think
perhaps if I could talk to the young man alone—

GEORGE [*doubtfully*]:   Well . . .

EDDIE: Aw—let him. He's not going to tell *us* anything.

WATCHMAN: He might get violent, Mr. Varity.

VARITY: No—I doubt that—

WATCHMAN: Well—we'll be back there, just in case—
[*He motions to the L*]

GEORGE: Okay. [*to* ALBERT] Tell Mr. Varity what's on
your mind, Albert. On account of we'd like to square
this thing with the front office—

ALBERT: The hell with the front office—

EDDIE: Sure . . . [*he sighs*] That's the most expensive
remark in the world, kid. Only the Chase National
Bank can make it. [*to* GEORGE] Come on—leave him
alone—

GEORGE [*leaving*]:   Take it easy, Albert.

[*They go off.* VARITY *draws out a cigarette, and offers
one to* ALBERT, *who refuses gloomily.* VARITY *lights up,
and regards him curiously. He half sits on the table.*]

VARITY: I am greatly interested in people who seek the truth, Albert. It is an old foible of mine. Was it the little lady from the commissary, perhaps, who did not tell you the truth? [ALBERT *nods miserably*] I thought as much. That is why I thought I would speak to you alone. I do not like the human race, Albert; they are monsters. Everybody who tries to help them—to teach them something—they have their foot on his neck. Paracelsus, Galileo, Copernicus—Lucifer . . . [*he sighs, and spreads his hands*] . . . even Lucifer.

ALBERT: She shouldn't have lied to me. I could take anything but being lied to—

VARITY: A lie is a very peculiar thing, my friend; if it is a good lie, it must distract you—so then you are not even sure that you have been lied to. Of course, she may be a bad liar; but even in that case, she does it for you—because if she does not care for you, she does not go to the trouble of making up falsehoods—she tells the truth. Which would have been—what?

ALBERT [*miserably*]:   That's just it. I don't know . . . But I can guess.

VARITY: Can you? Then you are a better guesser than I am. And I have been in the business much longer than you. To guess what a woman does—or why she does it—that is something for Einstein. Not even Einstein . . . Perhaps she wanted to find out something—about herself.

ALBERT: All right—so she's found out. She's a tramp.

VARITY: Maybe she found out just the opposite! That

she is *not* a tramp. Suppose the young lady has been—
asleep, shall we say? And the man comes—with fire
and passion—to wake her. And she does not wake!
[ALBERT *begins to weep*] On the contrary—she sleeps
more soundly than ever. That is no tramp—who does
not waken to the kiss of a stranger.

ALBERT [*weeping*]:   Don't say that—

VARITY [*gently*]:   What shall I say, then? We are mostly
strangers to each other, here on earth—

[ANNA *comes in quickly, R. She goes up to* VARITY, *and
faces him angrily, like an aroused mother-hen.*]

ANNA: What are you doing to him?

VARITY [*taken aback*]:   We are talking—

ANNA: Look at him! Aren't you ashamed—making him
cry!

[*She goes over and puts her arm around* ALBERT's *shoulders.*]

VARITY: *He* is the one to be ashamed. Besides—

ALBERT [*moving out of her arm*]:   Leave me alone!

ANNA: You hush now, Albert, and let me attend to this.
[*to* VARITY] How much trouble are they going to let
you make around here?

VARITY [*on the defensive*]:   Me? *He* is the one . . .

ANNA: A grown man like you!

ALBERT [*bitterly, to* ANNA]:   I don't need your help,
thank you—

ANNA [*she puts her hand back on his shoulder*]:   I know
what you think of me, Albert—you think I'm no good;
but it doesn't matter. Because there are some things

a girl finds out for herself—about the kind of person she is. And if she—likes somebody, she finds that out, too, for herself. That's all that matters, once you've found out.

VARITY: You surprise me, Anna—

ANNA: You leave him alone, that's all!

VARITY [*wondering*]:   *Now* you are lit up—like a pin-ball machine. But not before . . .

[*He shakes his head in wonder.*]

ANNA: Never mind how I was before.

VARITY: Like a pin-ball machine. All fire and light . . . what a story! I wouldn't have believed it.

ANNA [*with a fiercely tender maternal gesture, she draws* ALBERT'S *head in to her stomach*]:   I can tell a few stories, too, if I want to—

VARITY [*smiling a little*]:   So? Blackmail?

ANNA [*she looks at* VARITY *coolly*]:   A woman is what life makes her. [*turning to* ALBERT] It's all right, Albert. No one is going to do anything to you . . . while I can help it.

VARITY [*half to himself*]:   Well, well! I suppose I should be pleased to think that you could make trouble for my old antagonist upstairs . . . but do you know, I do not seem to care any more. [*rising*] Anyway, I wasn't altogether wrong . . . When a woman is aroused, watch out! . . . [*to* ANNA] Did I say something to you once about glory, and the morning sun? Well . . . enjoy it, my dear, enjoy it. [*to* ALBERT] You will be all right, Albert. You will not live any longer in

Eden, but you will populate the earth. [*ruefully*] I am sorry for you.

[*He goes out L, smiling, holding his finger to his lips as a signal to the others.* ANNA *stands stonily watching him.*]

ALBERT [*raising his head, and wiping his eyes*]:   Anna—did you—really? You know—

ANNA [*firmly*]:   I'd rather not discuss it, Albert.

ALBERT [*meekly*]:   Okay, Anna.

ANNA [*scornfully*]:   Anyway—what do men know about Eden?

[*As she stands protectively above him, the* CURTAIN QUICKLY FALLS.]

A NOTE ON THE TYPE

The text of this book is set in Caledonia, a Lino-type face designed by W. A. Dwiggins. Caledonia belongs to the family of printing types called "modern face" by printers—a term used to mark the change in style of type-letters that occurred about 1800. Caledonia borders on the general design of Scotch Modern, but is more freely drawn than that letter.

The book was composed, printed, and bound by Kingsport Press, Inc., Kingsport, Tennessee.